CW00832841

TRUE CRIME CASE HISTORIES

VOLUME 4

JASON NEAL

IDIGITAL GROUP

Cover photos of:

Austin Sigg (top-left)

Jennifer Pan (top-right)

Denise Williams (bottom-left)

Steven Pladl (bottom-right)

More books by Jason Neal

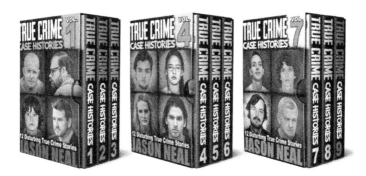

Looking for more?? I am constantly adding new volumes of True Crime Case Histories. The series **can be read in any order**, and all books are available in paperback, hardcover, and audiobook.

Check out the complete series at:

https://amazon.com/author/jason-neal

All Jason Neal books are also available in **AudioBook format at Audible.com.** Enjoy a **Free Audiobook** when you signup for a 30-Day trial using this link:

https://geni.us/AudibleTrueCrime

FREE BONUS EBOOK FOR MY READERS

As my way of saying "Thank you" for downloading, I'm giving away a FREE True Crime e-book I think you'll enjoy.

https://TrueCrimeCaseHistories.com

Just visit the link above to let me know where to send your free book!

CONTENTS

Introduction   ix

1. The Broomstick Killer   1
2. Bloodthirsty Parolee   17
3. The Body in the Bag   35
4. Mr. Mom Killer   49
5. The Incest Killer   69
6. The Copper Gulch Killer   77
7. Taking a Chance   87
8. The Tiger Parents   99
9. Mom, I'm a Monster   113
10. A Grisly New Orleans Tale   125
11. The Alligator Theory   133
12. The Kičevo Monster   145
13. Bonus Chapter: The Homeschoolers   155

Online Appendix   169
Also by Jason Neal   171
Free Bonus Book   173
Thank You!   175
About the Author   177

INTRODUCTION

If you've read the previous volumes of the True Crime Case Histories series, you know that I like to start with a brief word of warning. The stories included in this book are truly depraved and shocking. They are not for the squeamish. Many true crime television shows and news articles often leave out the gruesome details, simply because they may be too much for the average viewer or reader. With my books, I try not to leave out the details, no matter how vicious they may be. My intention is not to shock, but to provide a clear and accurate description of some of the most evil minds of the world. Though the stories are brief, I do my best to include enough detail so that the reader can get a better look into the demented mind of the killer.

This volume features twelve of the most incomprehensible stories of the last sixty years. Trying to understand the motivation behind murders like these can be an exercise in futility. But one thing is for sure—the stories in this volume will keep you turning pages.

In this book you'll encounter a story that has haunted me since I was a little kid growing up in southwest Washington. I lived a normal American life where I could ride my bike around my small town from dusk till dawn without a care in the world. When I was twelve years old, a boy in my neighborhood just a year older than I disappeared and was later found murdered. At the time I didn't know many of the details, but after researching the story all these years later and realizing that monsters like Tommy Ragan were roaming my tiny town, I may not have felt quite so secure.

In this volume you'll also read of how the Texas justice system grossly failed to protect the people of Texas. The result of their leniency was that a brutal killer of three teenagers was allowed back on the streets to kill as many as eleven more women.

Several of the stories include familial killings: There's the husband that killed his successful wife because he was jealous of her career, the wife that killed her husband so she could marry his best friend and collect insurance money, the young New Orleans man that survived Hurricane Katrina only to kill and cook his girlfriend, the young girl that hired hitmen to kill her parents, and the man that married his teenage daughter before hunting her down and killing her.

Though all the killings are senseless, some are particularly perplexing: One example is the story of the newspaper reporter who kidnapped, tortured, and butchered women who resembled his mother, then wrote stories of the killings in his newspaper articles. There's also the unthinkable story of a teenage boy obsessed with decomposition, who kidnapped, raped, and dismembered a young innocent girl.

The stories in this volume are revolting and disconcerting, but they're true. These things really happen in the world.

Though we will never fully understand the criminal mind, at least we can be better informed.

Lastly, please join my mailing list for discounts, updates, and a free book. You can sign up for that at

TrueCrimeCaseHistories.com

Additional photos, videos, and documents pertaining to the cases in this volume can be found on the accompanying web page:

https://TrueCrimeCaseHistories.com/vol4/

Thank you for reading. I sincerely hope you gain some insight from this volume of True Crime Case Histories.

- Jason

CHAPTER 1
THE BROOMSTICK KILLER

The tale of The Broomstick Killer is easily one of the most sinister stories in Texan history. Kenneth McDuff was a bloodthirsty killer who was granted unprecedented leniency by a justice system that allowed him to continue killing even after he had shown that he was a sadistic psychopath.

———

The tiny town of Rosebud in central Texas was the home of a notoriously strange family: the McDuffs. J.A. McDuff, the father, owned a cement finishing business that did quite well during the building boom of the late seventies, and the family was well-off by small town standards. The mother, Addie McDuff, ran the laundromat across from their home and doted over her six children. She was a large, headstrong woman known for being over-protective of her children, and would come running if they ever encountered trouble.

Addie was notoriously known to carry a gun in her purse and was referred to as the "Pistol-Packin' Mama" by the locals in Rosebud. Her children's teachers feared her because she would storm into the school in a huff any time one of her children was accused of misconduct. To Addie, her children could do no wrong whatsoever, and if someone accused them of anything, the school was likely to blame.

The eldest son, Lonnie, was the bully of the family. He once pulled a knife on the school principal who subsequently threw him down a flight of stairs. Lonnie spoke with a speech impediment and referred to himself as "Wuff and Tuff Wonnie McDuff."

Addie McDuff was particularly fond of her youngest son, Kenneth. Though technically he wasn't the youngest of the children, she fawned over him as her "baby boy." Even in his early teens when Kenneth started getting into trouble, somebody else was always to blame in her eyes.

Kenneth was a known troublemaker and a bully like his older brother Lonnie. He was always the kid with a pocketful of money, and new clothes, and he rode a loud motorcycle to school. Though he had an average IQ, he didn't do well in school. Kenneth didn't seem to care about school and his only genuine friend was his brother Lonnie.

By the fall of 1964 Kenneth was seventeen and spent most of his time causing trouble. He broke into businesses and homes looking for things to steal and drove around town looking for girls. But he wasn't looking for a girl to date: He was looking for a girl to rape. McDuff confided in his brother that he had once raped a woman, slit her throat, and left her dying. Whether the story was authentic is uncertain, as the crime was never reported.

Even at an early age, local law enforcement was all too familiar with Kenneth McDuff. Inevitably he was arrested in 1965 for a string of more than a dozen burglaries. The sentence for his crimes totaled fifty-two years, but because he was only eighteen the judge was lenient. McDuff was allowed to serve his time concurrently instead of consecutively. The fifty-two years of prison was reduced to a meager three years, and he only ended up serving ten months before they released him.

The brief sentence gave McDuff a sense of invincibility and just eight months later he moved on to much more heinous crimes.

On a hot August night in 1966, McDuff and his new friend Roy Dale Green were on their way to Fort Worth. Roy assumed they were on their way to drink some beer and look for girls, but McDuff had much more diabolical plans in mind.

Roy Dale Green was a skinny eighteen-year-old who was impressed with, and excited to be hanging out with twenty-year-old McDuff. Green knew that McDuff was a trouble-maker, but when Kenneth told him he wanted to rape a girl that night, Roy didn't take him seriously. When McDuff pulled into the parking lot of the baseball field in Everman, Texas, Roy had no idea what a mess he had got himself into.

McDuff pulled his car up next to a parked car near the baseball diamond; he could see there were three teenagers inside the car. He reached under the seat and pulled out a Colt .38 revolver, got out of the car, and walked up to the driver's side door of the parked car.

Pointing the revolver at the window, McDuff ordered the three teens out of the car. Inside the car was sixteen-year-old

Edna Louise Sullivan, her boyfriend seventeen-year-old Robert Brand, and his fifteen-year-old cousin Mark Dunham. McDuff led them to the trunk of the car and commanded them to get in. The three teens climbed in, and he closed the lid.

McDuff drove their car while Roy Green followed in McDuff's car to an isolated area where they stopped. McDuff and Green got out of the cars and McDuff turned to Green and said, "We're gonna have to knock 'em off." Kenneth then opened the trunk and pulled Edna out. The teen girl screamed as he dragged her away from her friends to his own car and locked her in his trunk. He then went back over to the young boys. Unable to see, Edna's terror only intensified when she heard six gunshots. McDuff had emptied the revolver into the two other boys' bodies. When he could not close the trunk, McDuff became frustrated and backed the car up to a fence and abandoned it with the boy's bodies hanging out of the back.

Roy Green was in shock. They both got back in to McDuff's car and drove to another location where McDuff pulled Edna out of the back of the car and raped her. After he raped her, McDuff ordered Green to rape her too. Then McDuff yelled to Green, "Find something for me to strangle her with." Green pulled the belt off of his pants and handed it to him, but McDuff found something he liked better. He had a broom in the back of his car. He raped her with the broomstick, then sat on her chest and held it across her neck. He leaned forward on the broomstick, putting more and more pressure on her neck until he crushed her throat. McDuff threw her body over his shoulder, walked to the side of the dirt road and tossed her body into the nearby bushes; the two drove away.

The next day Roy Green was consumed with guilt and told his friend's mother what they had done. His friend's mother went to Green's mother, who subsequently convinced him to turn himself in.

Green was arrested and led the police to the bodies, and McDuff was quickly arrested as well. Green gave the police the gun that McDuff had buried next to his garage.

During the trial, a terrified Roy Green stuttered and stammered as he testified against McDuff. McDuff was cocky and nonchalant, taking the stand in his own defense, but it didn't help his case.

In November 1966 a jury found Kenneth McDuff guilty on three counts of murder. Roy Green served eleven years in prison for his part in the murders, while McDuff was handed three death sentences in the electric chair. In a normal world, this would be the end of the story, but it was nowhere near over.

On June 29, 1972 after six years on death row, the US Supreme Court decided that the death penalty, as it was then written, was a cruel and unusual punishment and was therefore unconstitutional under the Eighth and Fourteenth Amendments. In an extraordinary event, all death penalty cases in the United States were commuted to life sentences.

McDuff was now eligible for parole and applied for it every time he was allowed. He was convicted of such heinous crimes; it was unimaginable that he would ever be paroled. The residents of Central Texas thought that such a vicious killer could never be paroled. Over and over he applied, and he was repeatedly denied.

Fifteen years later in 1987, McDuff saw his chance. The Texas Federal Court ruled that the prisons of Texas were far too overcrowded, violating the civil rights of the inmates. Rather than spend money building more prisons, the courts set population limits in the prisons which led to a massive backlog of inmates being held in county jails across the state.

Texas Governor Bill Clements made an unthinkable deal with the parole board. In order to reduce prison population, they were required to release 150 inmates per day. Initially, the white-collar crimes were released, then the minor drug offenses. Within two years the only people left in the prisons were murderers. This is when McDuff saw his chance.

Each time he applied for parole, McDuff still had to appear before a parole board of three members, plead his case, and get two out of three votes in his favor. He had tried several times and was denied each time. In one instance he actually received two votes, but it was ultimately denied when an unknown party argued against his release. In another instance he tried to bribe a parole board official by offering him $10,000. Each time he was denied, but it didn't deter him.

Outside of the prison, McDuff's mother was busy doing her part. She hired two well-known attorneys from Huntsville, paying them $2,200 to try to find a way to get her beloved son released from prison.

Unbelievably, in 1989, after serving twenty-three years in prison, McDuff was paroled. The two members of the parole board that voted to release him were James Granberry and Chris Mealy. Mealy later blamed the tremendous pressure he was under from the government. Granberry was later charged with perjury in an unrelated case and ordered to serve six months in a halfway house.

During those years, the Texas parole board set free 127 murderers and twenty death row inmates.

———

The people of Rosebud were in shock at the news of McDuff's release. Some put bars over their windows and many feared walking the streets of the tiny town without a gun.

Immediately after his release, McDuff was required to visit his parole officer in Temple, Texas. After their first visit, the parole officer told police,

> "I don't know if it'll be next week or next month or next year, but one of these days, dead girls are gonna start turning up, and when that happens, the man you need to look for is Kenneth McDuff."

The parole officer was right. Just three days after his release, the body of twenty-nine-year-old Sarafia Parker was found in a field twenty-five miles west of Rosebud in Temple, the town that McDuff's parents had moved to while he was in prison. Though they had no evidence, police suspected McDuff was responsible for the killing.

McDuff was known as a racist. Just seven months after his release he harassed a young black man in Rosebud, yelling racial slurs at him, and pulled a knife on him. This violated his parole, and he was quickly sent back to prison, but McDuff knew how the prison system worked. He knew about the overcrowding issues and he was back on the streets just two months later.

After his release from prison, McDuff enrolled at Texas State Technical College in Waco and briefly got a job as a cashier at a convenience store called Quik-Pak. But working for a lowly $4 an hour did not satisfy him, and he quit after only a month.

By the summer of 1991, McDuff had given up his feeble attempts at the straight-and-narrow life and continued his life of crime. Living in the college dorms, he started dealing and using drugs. He knew this violated his parole, but he didn't care. He spent his spare time picking up prostitutes in Waco and used them to satisfy his need for violent sex.

In the late hours of October 10, 1991, McDuff picked up a young crack-addicted prostitute from Waco, Brenda Thompson, intent on killing her. McDuff had Brenda tied up in the passenger seat of his red pickup truck when he noticed a police checkpoint up ahead. Brenda saw her opportunity and screamed as she raised her legs up to the windshield and began kicking, cracking the windshield several times. When the police ran toward his truck McDuff hit the gas and crashed the roadblock. Several police officers had to jump out of the way to avoid being run over.

McDuff led police on a high-speed chase but escaped into the night by turning off his lights and driving the wrong way down one-way streets. After he escaped, he took Brenda Thompson down an old abandoned road into a wooded area near Route 84 where he raped, tortured, and murdered her. Her body wasn't found until seven years later.

Just a week later McDuff picked up another Waco prostitute. Seventeen-year-old Regina DeAnne Moore was last seen arguing outside a motel with McDuff on the night of October 17. Again, McDuff tied her arms and legs with her own stockings, then took her to a remote area where he raped and murdered her. Her remains were not found until 1998.

Two months later in Austin, twenty-eight-year-old Colleen Reed was washing her shiny new Mazda Miata convertible at a self-serve car wash.

One thing that McDuff learned in prison was to find a malleable sidekick. That evening he was driving around Austin with his latest sidekick, Alva Hank Worley. As they drove past the car wash McDuff spotted Colleen and made a quick U-turn.

McDuff pulled his tan Thunderbird into the bay next to hers, got out of the car and walked into Colleen's stall. Without a word, McDuff grabbed her around the neck and lifted the tiny girl off the ground. When Colleen screamed, neighbors behind the car wash came out to see what was happening. They watched as McDuff threw Colleen in his car and he and Worley drove away, again driving the wrong way on a one-way street.

The witnesses got a good look at Worley and alerted the police of his description and the type and color of the vehicle that sped away. Right away police suspected that McDuff was behind the abduction.

When police got the description of Worley, they began looking through McDuff's known associates and noticed Hank Worley immediately as one of his known drinking buddies. Like Roy Dale Green, Worley was timid and easily influenced by McDuff.

Worley wasn't hard to find, living in a motel with his four-teen-year-old daughter. When police knocked on his door, he was already terrified with guilt.

Though his guilt consumed him, he feared McDuff and wasn't quite ready to point a finger at him. On the first visit to his motel room, Worley claimed he barely knew McDuff. It took a few visits to his motel room for police to persuade him to admit to what had happened that night. They stopped by while he was having a barbecue by the motel pool with his daughter, and Detective Mike McNamara whispered in his ear,

> "Hank, you're hiding a kid killer, you know that? You're protecting a man who raped and brutalized and strangled a girl not much older than your daughter over there. Picture her on the ground, a broomstick across her throat, crying out for you to help, begging you to speak out, to do what's right, to save the life of some young girl, to…"

McNamara couldn't finish his sentence before Worley screamed. He was ready to talk. When investigators got him into the interrogation room, he told the complete story of the night of Colleen's abduction.

Worley said he and McDuff were in Austin looking for drugs when McDuff saw Colleen washing her car. When McDuff lifted her off the ground by her throat she screamed "Please, not me! Not me!" He then threw her in the back of their car and told Worley to hold her down as they sped off.

When they got a few miles out of Austin McDuff got in the back with Colleen and commanded Worley to keep driving out of town. McDuff tied her hands behind her back with her shoelaces, then took his cigarette and put it out between her legs as she screamed. He beat her and raped her. When he finished, he told Worley to change places with him and Worley raped her while McDuff drove.

Worley recalled, "I didn't want to have sex with her but if I didn't have sex with her, I knew that he was gonna get back there with her and beat her up some more and burn her with cigarettes. He was taking the cigarettes and getting the fire real hot and burning her down there in the wrong spots."

When they got near the town of Belton, McDuff pulled onto a secluded dirt road and raped her again.

"He turned around, and he hit her. Slapped her real hard and knocked her backwards. Then he took another cigarette, and he lit it, and got the fire real hot and he burned her like that again."

When she was able to stand Worley claimed Colleen put her head on his shoulder and said "Please don't let him hurt me anymore." McDuff was having none of that. He grabbed her by the neck and stuffed her into the trunk of the car and turned to Worley and said, "I'm gonna use her up." McDuff used the term often to mean that he was going to terminate her life.

"Then he put her in the trunk of the car, closed the trunk down and he takes me home. On the way home he asked me for my pocketknife and I told him I don't know where it is."

"Then he asked me, 'Well, I need a shovel. Let me borrow a shovel.' And I said, 'I ain't got one.' He didn't say what he was going to do with it, but I knew what he was gonna do with it. He wanted to kill her with it."

"Ain't nothin' I could do. Real scary being like that. If you can't help yourself, there ain't no way you gonna help anybody else. I wasn't even sure if I was gonna make it outta that."

"I'll always have a tear for that girl. I'll always cry for her, for what she went through. Nobody should be put through that type of torture."

McDuff was nowhere to be found, but police knew he was still in the area the following February when they found the body of another young prostitute. Twenty-two-year-old Valencia Joshua, a student at the same college that McDuff had attended was found on a golf course near the school. She had been strangled. The last time anyone had seen her, she was looking for Kenneth McDuff on the campus of their school.

Then on March 1, 1992, Melissa Northrup was working the night-shift at the Quik-Pak convenience store. She was a pregnant mother of two who knew the dangers of working the night shift, but needed to pay the bills. She would regularly call her husband during her shift to let him know she was okay.

Late that night McDuff was cruising the streets looking for drugs when his tan Thunderbird broke down just 100 yards from the Quik-Pak. This was the same store that McDuff had worked for only a month. McDuff knew that the store was open twenty-four hours a day and had no security to speak of. He also knew that there was a cute twenty-three-year-old who worked the night shift and had told friends that the place could easily be robbed.

When Melissa's husband didn't hear from her at 4:00 a.m. that night he got worried and called the store. He repeatedly got no answer so he drove to the store, but there was no sign of his wife.

When police found McDuff's car abandoned at the New Road Inn just 100 yards away, their suspicions were confirmed. McDuff was on a killing spree, and they started a massive nationwide manhunt.

Knowing how close McDuff was with his family, they started by questioning his parents. As always, his mother stood by her beloved son and claimed he was innocent but didn't know where he was. His father, however, was less loving,

> "I don't know where he is. If you find him, you can kill him if you want to."

On April 26, the badly decomposed body of Quik-Pak employee Melissa Northrup was found floating in a gravel quarry in Dallas County. Her hands were still tied behind her back with shoelaces - a signature of Kenneth McDuff.

The big break came on May 1 when the manhunt was aired on America's Most Wanted. The TV show was massively popular; through the years it has helped capture 1,200 fugitives. This airing was no exception. Shortly after it aired a man called from Kansas City, Missouri claiming that McDuff worked for a trash company under the assumed name Richard Fowler.

Texas police called Kansas City police who looked up the name Richard Fowler in their records. Someone had been using the name and had been arrested and fingerprinted for soliciting prostitutes. The fingerprints matched that of Kenneth McDuff. McDuff was arrested on May 4, 1992 as he was driving a trash truck to a landfill.

When he was brought back to Texas, crowds of angry people gathered outside of the courthouse. McDuff embraced the media and professed his innocence to the mob of cameras outside, often claiming that his trial was unfair.

Prosecutors had their strongest evidence against him for the abduction and murder of Melissa Northrup, so they decided to try that case first and worry about the rest later.

Addie McDuff, who was now seventy-seven years old, was called as a hostile witness to testify against her son. She confirmed that her son used her credit card near the Quik-Pak store on the night of the abduction, putting him near the scene of the crime when it happened.

McDuff was livid that his own mother was being used by the prosecution to testify against him, but there was more to come. The prosecution called two of his friends to testify that he had tried to enlist them in his plans to rob the Quik-Pak store.

At one point McDuff directed his anger at his own attorneys when he screamed at them,

> "Why don't you get up and go sit on the prosecution's side! You're helping them more than you are me!"

The murder of Colleen Reed had not been tried yet, and the prosecution called Hank Worley to testify to show that there was a signature to McDuff's killings. Worley was brought to the courthouse in handcuffs. From his visible shaking, it was clear that just being in the presence of McDuff again terrified him.

The ultimate nail in the coffin for McDuff was when he insisted on testifying on his own behalf despite his defense team's wishes. They explained to him that under the rules of evidence, his past 1966 murders couldn't be mentioned in court if he wasn't on the stand, but if he took the stand, the prosecution could use that against him. McDuff wouldn't listen.

McDuff took the stand for two hours rambling a nonsensical story of his whereabouts on the night of the murder. Meanwhile, the prosecution took advantage of their opportunity and the jury heard the complete story of his brutal killings of the teenagers in 1966.

The jury took four hours to return their guilty verdict on February 16, 1993. His defense team requested leniency and asked for a life sentence, but the jury only took one hour to decide that Kenneth McDuff should die by lethal injection.

McDuff's trial for the murder of Colleen Reed started in 1994. Although the body had still not been found, he was given a second death sentence.

In television interviews from prison awaiting his death sentence, McDuff continued to profess his innocence, even for the 1966 killings.

In the months before his execution, investigators enlisted the help of a jailhouse informant to try to get McDuff to give up the locations of the bodies. Their plan worked.

In September 1998, the body of Regina DeAnne Moore was found beneath a bridge on the side of a highway. McDuff had buried her in a shallow grave. Her hands were still tied behind her back with shoelaces, and her ankles were bound with stockings.

The body of Brenda Thompson, who kicked McDuff's windshield as he crashed through the roadblock, was found in a grouping of trees outside of Waco. She had been tied up, raped, and tortured.

McDuff only had two weeks before his execution, but he wasn't giving up the location of Colleen Reed. He told the informant that he didn't want to tell the cops because it was the last body and if he gave them everything they needed they would "take away my commissary rights, and won't treat me right." With only two weeks to live, McDuff's only concern was his own diminished rights and had no regard for the closure of his victim's families.

Police met with prison officials and arranged to take none of his prison rights away. Presented with the assurance, McDuff finally gave them directions to where he had buried Colleen Reed's body.

Despite digging for hours exactly where he told them, they were unable to locate her body. That afternoon, in a covert arrangement, McDuff was brought to the dig site. The body of Colleen Reed was found on October 6, 1998.

In McDuff's final days investigator John Moriarty spent over forty hours interviewing him, trying to gain a deeper understanding of the psychopath's mind. In the time he spent with him, though he showed no remorse at all, McDuff admitted to all eight murders and alluded that there may have been many more.

Kenneth McDuff was executed on November 17, 1998. His family didn't claim his body, and he was buried in the Huntsville prison graveyard with a tombstone that displayed only his death row number X999055 and the day of execution.

As a result of the mayhem that McDuff caused and an outcry from the public, the Texas parole system was completely overhauled and the state spent $2 billion building more prisons.

CHAPTER 2
BLOODTHIRSTY
PAROLEE

Anyone who has driven the 180 mile stretch of Interstate 5 from Portland, Oregon to Seattle, Washington possibly remembers the small town of Centralia, Washington. Not because it's of particularly any historical importance—though it has plenty of history—but mostly it's because it's the halfway point between Portland and Seattle and a convenient place to stop for gas or to grab some fast food.

In 1977 Centralia was a town of only 10,000 residents and neighboring Chehalis had only about 5,000. Together they were known as the Twin Cities. It was a beautiful rural area surrounded by miles and miles of dense forest in every direction.

The story of the murder of thirteen-year-old Bruce Kim is almost entirely absent on the internet. I only know of the story because I lived only a few blocks from Bruce and he was just a few years older than me. Though we lived close to each other, I barely knew the boy; Bruce had an entirely separate circle of friends. Though only thirteen, like many other kids in the seventies, Bruce got involved with the wrong crowd.

On the evening of New Year's Day in 1977 Bruce Kim attended a house party at number 7 in the Lemac Apartments, an old, run-down apartment building near the railroad tracks at the north end of town. The resident of apartment number 7 was an older man who was known to have parties to which anyone could come, drink, party, or buy some weed or LSD—regardless of age.

On New Year's Day, friends had seen Bruce riding his bicycle on the streets of Centralia, but that evening he didn't return home after the party. The next morning Bruce's mother, Joan, called the Centralia police,

> "He has never stayed out overnight without calling me. He wouldn't have gone away willingly."

Bruce's bicycle was in front of their house at 1002 L Street, but he was nowhere to be found. Bruce was small for his age and had long reddish-brown hair. The last anyone had seen him he was wearing blue jeans, a jean jacket, and a printed t-shirt. There were no clothes missing from his closet and he had very little money to his name, so police ruled out the chance that he had simply run away from home.

Local detectives immediately contacted Bruce's closest friends to try to backtrack his last known events. That's when they found out that he had attended the party in the Lemac Apartments.

Detectives spoke to the resident of the apartment who gave police a list of attendees of the party as best he could remember. They then spent the next few days tracking down the attendees and questioning them one by one. Unfortunately, the apartment was a known drug den and most of the party-goers that attended weren't too excited to speak to police. The interviews uncovered no new clues in tracking down the boy.

Just before midnight on January 6, a man ran to the Centralia fire department and pounded on the locked doors. It was late, and nobody was answering. He had just run six blocks from the Lemac Apartments, which was engulfed in flames. Frustrated, he ran another three blocks to the police department who then alerted the fire department. By the time firetrucks arrived at the Lemac Apartments, it was too late. By morning the building was nothing but charred black sticks and rubble.

When the fire marshal assessed the damage, at first glance it seemed clean. There was no evidence of accelerants. The building was very old and had archaic wiring so the chance of the cause of the fire being faulty wiring was high, but intuition told him it was more than that. He suspected an experienced arsonist. When the fire marshal heard that the building was the last place Bruce Kim was seen alive, it only solidified his suspicions. The cause of fire was initially determined to be inconclusive.

Centralia detectives told reporters,

> "If Bruce Kim's body had been in the apartment, there would have been some evidence of his remains in the fire debris. Fragments of bone... something. It is extremely rare for a body to be completely destroyed in a fire, even a Holocaust as fully involved as that of the Lemac."

As the days passed police grew frustrated at the lack of clues, but on January 13 their luck turned. A woman named Susan

Ragan called the county Sheriff and told him she had something to show him. The woman told him that Bruce Kim was most likely dead and showed him a pair of blue jeans that her brother had left with her. The cuffs of the jeans were stained with what appeared to be blood. She was holding the jeans for her brother, and she was clearly terrified.

> The lead investigator recalled, "She says Tommy brought her the jeans and told her he'd gotten the stains on the cuffs when he'd turned a body over with his foot."

Susan Regan was the sister of thirty-three-year-old Tommy Regan, a name that was well known to the Centralia Police and the Lewis County Sheriff. Tommy's conflicts with police dated back to his teenage years.

———

Even as a teenager Tommy Ragan was in trouble with the law. At fifteen years old Ragan had stolen a car and was confined to the Green Hill School, Washington's maximum security lockup for older juveniles. One night Ragan and another young inmate broke out of the school, stole a 1.5 ton vehicle, and went on a rampage. The two went the wrong way up the highway, crashing through a police barricade, ramming six other cars and almost running over a police officer. They led police on a forty-five mile high-speed pursuit before they were finally stopped.

Over the next seventeen years Ragan spent more time in prison than out with charges ranging from burglary, larceny, and car theft, to rape and kidnapping.

The worst of his offenses was when he was twenty years old. Ragan was charged with kidnapping a fourteen-year-old boy named Bobby at knifepoint. Ragan approached two young boys after a baseball game in Fort Borst Park and asked for help to push his car. When they started pushing Ragan pulled a switch-blade knife on them. One boy ran away, but Ragan grabbed Bobby and dragged him into the forest, cutting him several times in the ribs with the knife. Once in the forest he sodomized the boy and dragged him across the Skookumchuck River. The boy that got away had alerted police and Bobby was able to get away when Ragan was distracted by police sirens.

At the time, Ragan was only charged with kidnapping, but years later the boy confided the entire story to police that he was orally and anally raped by Ragan at knifepoint. Coincidentally Bobby went on to be one of Centralia's few celebrities, playing Major League Baseball for five years.

At the time of Bruce Kim's disappearance, Tommy Ragan was out on parole. His address at the time was ninety miles away in Seattle, but he had been visiting family in Centralia. Ragan had also been an attendee at the party in the Lemac apartments, in fact police had questioned him in the days after. Detectives were very keen to question him further since they had the additional information about the bloody jeans.

Detectives needed to find Tommy Ragan. According to his parole officer in Seattle, he was living with someone named Christina Keithana Kempf. Christina's past was every bit as sordid as Ragan's. She was actually born Charles Wheeler. At an early age he realized that he had a boy's body but identified as a girl.

"All I knew was I wanted to be a girl… and I wasn't."

In his teens Charles assumed he was just gay. He was married at sixteen but was divorced by twenty-one.

> "The homosexual life was a disappointment, I wanted to talk love and marriage, pots and pans, and they wanted to talk sex."

After the divorce, Charles turned to alcohol and entered a traumatic depression that landed him in the Easter State Mental Hospital with a diagnosis of incipient schizophrenia. Upon release from the hospital, Charles decided to become Christine. She changed her name and started wearing women's clothes and makeup. She desperately wanted to make it official by getting a sex change, but she lacked the funds for the expensive procedure.

It wasn't long before Christina was arrested and sentenced to twenty years in prison for cashing stolen checks, but was released after only three years.

Within twenty days of her release, she was arrested again. This time for murder. According to Christina, she was accosted in the parking lot of a grocery store by a man that was trying to force her to have sex. During the altercation, she stabbed the man to death.

Christina was sentenced to life in prison in the Washington State Penitentiary in Walla Walla—a men's prison. Identifying as a woman, she was harassed in prison and ridiculed for being a cross-dresser. Prison psychologists criticized her, telling her that she was just homosexual.

Though she was sentenced to life in prison, she was released in 1973. Upon her release an anonymous donor had sent her $1,000 to start a fund to help her pay for a sex change. The anonymous donor ended up being an odd, flamboyant "church" in Seattle. The donation wasn't enough for a full sex change, so Christina got breast implants and started hormone therapy.

In the spring of 1973 Christina had married again. This time to a man named Andy. The wedding took place in a huge, opulent mansion on Lake Washington that was the head-quarters of the church that gave her the donation. The preacher of the church and owner of the mansion was a large, eccentric man with 40D fake breasts who dressed in flowing silk robes. The church televised their wedding and paid for their honeymoon in Hawaii.

The marital bliss didn't last long. Both Christina and Andy were arrested on drug charges and sentenced to prison. They arrested Christina as Charles Wheeler, and she shared a cell with her husband Andy.

After only eighteen months Christina was out of prison again and moved into an apartment in Seattle with Tommy Ragan while Andy still sat in jail.

———

On January 14, Centralia detectives were still searching for Tommy Ragan. They had pulled him over in his 1960 green Corvair on January 12 for a traffic violation, but that was before he was wanted for questioning and nobody had seen him since. In addition to the Corvair, Ragan often drove a brown 1965 Barracuda which belonged to Christina Kempf. Police were on the lookout for both vehicles, but were cautious knowing that he may be armed. It was rumored that Ragan often carried a sawed-off .22 caliber rifle.

The Seattle police were looking for Ragan too. Neither Christina nor Ragan were at their Seattle apartment.

That same day Centralia detectives went back to Ragan's sister's house to see if they could get any more information out of her and they were in luck. His sister was nothing like her brother. She didn't want any part of him if he had murdered a fourteen-year-old boy and told police exactly what Tommy had told her. She told police that Ragan admitted to her he had killed Bruce Kim. She said that Tommy told her he had buried the body somewhere near Yelm, Washington, a tiny town about thirty miles northeast of Centralia.

The problem was, Centralia was surrounded by dense forest, and Yelm was even more so. It would take a miracle to find a grave in such a vast wilderness without more specific information.

Centralia police contacted the Yelm police for help. Ragan had some prison buddies in the area that they thought he might stay with, but they hadn't heard from him.

When police checked on the status of the 1960 Corvair they saw that Ragan had just sold it the day before, January 13—the day after he had been pulled over for a traffic violation. Detectives contacted the new owners of the Corvair and impounded the vehicle. The new owners quickly stopped payment on the check that they wrote to Ragan before he could cash it.

Inside the car they found what looked like bloodstains on the seats and tiny bits of dirt. On the bottom side of the car they saw that the undercarriage had recently scraped something. Their assumption was that Ragan had bottomed out the car somewhere on an old logging trail in Yelm when he was disposing of the body.

That same evening, January 14, Seattle police found Ragan and took him into custody for breaking parole. On the ninety mile drive in the back of a patrol car back down to Centralia, he kept his mouth shut.

Ragan's sister was desperately trying to distance herself from her brother. She had very little doubt that her brother had killed the boy and she called police one more time. When detectives came to her house, she gave them two items that Tommy had left with her: A shovel still covered with dirt and a pocketknife.

She also had a little more information than she let on the first time. She told detectives that she didn't know the exact location that he had buried him, but said,

> "It's supposed to be near the Cougar Mountain area of Yelm. There's an old logging road, a mud hole where you have to turn and go through a fence—a kind of rise in the land as the road bends around. There're trees. Just small fir trees…"

Police hypothesized that the "rise in the land" was where Ragan may have bottomed out the Corvair. On the morning of January 16, a search team of officers scoured the area near Cougar Mountain. The January weather in southwest Washington was notoriously miserable, rainy, and wet making old logging roads muddy.

The terrain in the Yelm forest was filled with thick blackberry bushes, vines, and fir trees. Searching a forest so thick and overgrown was almost pointless, and the first day of the search was a failure.

The next day the crew searched again. This time they were armed with aerial maps of the area and plaster impressions they had taken from the Corvair tires. At a fork in an old logging road, they came across their first clue. A match in the mud to the Corvair tires.

They followed the Corvair tracks and further up the old road found a hump that could have caused the scratch marks on the bottom of the car. Detectives took dirt samples from the road, hoping they could later match it to the dirt found on the underside of the Corvair.

Where the tracks seemed to end, police spread out to search the dense forest. Most of the police in the area were also regular deer hunters and had a lot of experience rummaging through the thick woods.

About 100 feet into the forest from the logging road, one detective noticed a fallen tree that had recently been burned. He thought he may be onto something. There were also what seemed to be drag marks in the mud near the log.

Not far from the log he noticed a patch of buffalo grass. The grass wasn't planted in the ground though. It seemed as if it had been torn away and was lying on the ground. It was obvious that someone had intended to hide something beneath.

The team was called to the site, and they dug very lightly, using only their hands. The dirt was fresh and not packed down. Just six inches below the surface they reached flesh. As they pushed the dirt aside, they could tell it was the back and hip of a small person. Face down.

There were what appeared to be slashes and scratches across the back. As they cleared the dirt away from the rest of the body and reached the neck, they realized there was a massive gash, but nothing could prepare them for what they saw next. As they continued to dig they realized that it wasn't a gash at all. The head had been completely severed. There was no head at all in the grave.

When the decapitated body was pulled out of the shallow grave and laid on the ground, it was clear that someone had tried to dissect the limbs, but failed. Other joints were cut but not all the way through. Possibly the killer was unaware just how hard it is to dismember a body. When they rolled the body over onto its back they were in for another shock. They could tell that the body was male, but the genitals had been severed completely. Additionally, there was a massive gash from the pubic bone up to the chest.

As the day progressed, investigators painstakingly processed the crime scene, scouring the area for anything the killer may have left behind. All they found were some scraps of toilet paper with a distinctive brown floral print on them.

The body was taken back to Centralia, and they brought a forensic pathologist up from Portland, Oregon for the post-mortem examination. Although investigators knew this had to be the body of Bruce Kim, they would still need some confirmation of identity. The cold January weather was helpful as it had minimized decomposition.

Bruce had never been fingerprinted and since they didn't find a head buried with the body, they couldn't identify him by dental records. Just a year earlier, however, Bruce had suffered a severe leg break. When the body was X-rayed it showed the break. The break matched with the X-rays on file with Centralia General Hospital. It was indeed the body of Bruce Kim.

During the autopsy Bruce's blood alcohol level was read at .21, an impossibly high level for anyone, let alone a thirteen-year-old boy. Decomposition and the extreme blood loss can alter the reading though, so the pathologist wasn't sure that it was accurate.

Tommy Ragan was in lockup for parole violation, and he wasn't talking. Investigators then retraced all of his movements since the first of the year. They already knew that he was at the party at the Lemac Apartments. They also learned that he borrowed a shovel from a prison friend of his at 1:30 p.m. on January 3, returning it later that evening. They also learned that he had slept in Christina Kempf's Barracuda one block from the Lemac Apartments on the night of the fire. He had also been seen in the Yelm area near where the body was found on January 12.

Though they had found what they thought to be bloodstains and mud in the Corvair, none of that evidence was useable.

Christina Kempf was still nowhere to be found, and police desperately wanted to speak to her. They were unsure if Ragan may have had help with the murder.

On January 20, police got a warrant to search Ragan and Christina's apartment in Seattle and her Barracuda. Inside the apartment detectives found work gloves caked with dirt and maps of the Yelm area along with miscellaneous paperwork that belonged to Tommy. In the paperwork were several handwritten pages penned by Ragan. It was a story of a homosexual killing involving two killers and one victim.

They also found rolls of toilet paper with a brown floral print - exactly the same as the shreds they found near the gravesite.

The search warrant, however, was very specific and one detective spotted something that could be useful, but legally wasn't included in the warrant. They needed the signature from a Superior Court judge to get an additional warrant, but it was late at night. That night they found a judge to sign for a second warrant and went back to the apartment again.

The item they wanted was a photo they'd seen in a photo album. One picture in particular showed Ragan staring wide-eyed into the camera framing his face. On both cheeks were smears of red liquid that looked like blood in the shape of a pentagram - a five-pointed star pointed downward, often associated with the occult or devil worship. Investigators now questioned whether Bruce Kim had been murdered as part of some sort of cult ritual.

Detectives later questioned every tenant of the Seattle Apartment building. In that questioning they found that Christina owned a third car, a Toyota that was still sitting in the parking lot. With another warrant police searched the car and found pick axes, dirt, ropes, and an army shovel.

Another tenant told detectives that Christina had confided in them that Ragan had told her he accidentally hit a young boy with his car, breaking his neck. According to Christina, Ragan panicked and buried the boy. Police knew there was no truth in this story. Bruce's body had no broken bones and no bruising to indicate being hit by a car.

Detectives still needed to talk to Christina, but she was nowhere to be found. The next obvious person to talk to was the church minister who had conducted her wedding and paid for her breast implants and honeymoon to Hawaii.

When police arrived at the church minister's opulent mansion, it was clear they had stumbled onto a cult of sorts. It seemed that many people lived at the mansion with dramatic artwork, two-inch thick shag carpet and a view overlooking Lake Washington. Another thing they noticed right away was that the room they were in was the background in Ragan's pentagram photo. The picture had been taken there.

One of the women at the mansion remembered Ragan and said she was the person that took the photo of him. She claimed it was all just a joke, and she painted the pentagrams on his face. Ultimately, the residents barely remembered Ragan; they said they hadn't seen Christina in quite some time and had no idea where she might be.

In a strange coincidence, there was an article in the Sunday, January 30 edition of the Seattle newspaper about Christina. The article wasn't about the police search for her, but rather a sympathetic piece about the struggles with homosexual and transgender life featuring a photo of her lounging in silk pajamas showing her artificial cleavage. The newspaper had no idea about the search for her and her possible involvement in a horribly sadistic murder.

On February 8, Christina gave up hiding from police and walked into the police station with an attorney. She insisted she had nothing to do with the murder and had no knowledge of it at all and therefore could give no testimony. But when prosecutors offered her immunity to testify against Ragan, she quickly took it.

Tommy Ragan was initially charged with aggravated murder, meaning that a murder was committed in the course of or in furtherance of the crime of rape or kidnapping. It was the only crime in Washington state punishable with a mandatory death sentence. Prosecutors believed that Bruce had been sexually assaulted before he was killed and the death was an attempt to cover up the crime of rape.

Once Ragan was behind bars, detectives revisited Bobby, the young boy that had been kidnapped by Ragan thirteen years earlier. It was then that Bobby broke down and told police of the rape. He told detectives he was severely traumatized and thought of himself as lucky to be alive. He told detectives that Ragan took him into the woods, tied him up, put the switchblade to his throat and told him he would cut off his genitals if he wasn't cooperative. Even with Bobby's testimony, prosecutors knew that trying to prove aggravated murder would be a stretch.

When word got to the public that Ragan had been charged, another witness came forward. A man that was at the Lemac party in the early hours of January 2 told police that he saw Ragan having sex with Bruce Kim. Though this information didn't suggest the sex was forced and showed nothing to prove that Ragan murdered him, it still helped solidify the case.

The trial was set for late April, but just before the start date of the trial Ragan's attorney told police that he wanted to talk. Ragan and his attorney asked for a deal. Ragan offered to plead guilty to a lesser charge of second degree murder. To sweeten the deal, Ragan told detectives he would show them where he buried Bruce Kim's head.

Ragan had already been convicted of three felonies, making him a likely candidate to be "bitched," a slang term used to describe a habitual criminal. If prosecutors could get Ragan convicted as a habitual criminal he would be sentenced to life and would likely never be released.

On April 18, Ragan pleaded guilty to second degree murder and led detectives to the head of Bruce Kim. Investigators considered themselves lucky to find the body, but it would have taken a miracle to find the head on their own. The lead detective said it was,

"Buried in brush so thick a coyote wouldn't crawl through it."

The head was located in dense blackberry bushes about 300 yards from the gravesite. Using dental records, the identity was confirmed to be that of Bruce Kim. Ragan told police that he had thrown Bruce's clothes from the car as he was driving along the logging road. Backtracking the road, police found several pieces of his clothes.

Ragan then explained the details of the killing to detectives. He claimed that they both left the party at the Lemac Apartments and went to Bruce's house. They were both extremely drunk and Bruce swore at Ragan, which threw him into a rage. Ragan said he wrapped his hands around his neck and started to strangle the boy. Bruce was much smaller and younger than Ragan.

"I didn't realize I had killed him. I thought he was breathing."

When Ragan finally released his grip, it was too late. Bruce was dead. He said he then put Bruce's body into the trunk of the Corvair and drove to Seattle. Later he drove back down to Yelm and buried it. He told police he cut off his head at the gravesite to avoid identification.

When asked why he cut off Bruce's genitals and where they were, he had no recollection of it. He claimed to not remember anything about any additional mutilations, the slash marks, or the attempted dismemberments. Ragan insinuated that he must have blacked that out.

Because of the media attention in the Centralia area, Ragan's trial was moved from Lewis County to Pacific County. One evening when driving back to the Lewis County jail with the

Centralia Chief of police, they passed a familiar hamburger stand. Ragan lamented that he would probably never taste another milkshake for the rest of his life. Chief Jones was a firm believer that all men deserved some sense of dignity, regardless of what they may have done in their lives. He stopped by the drive-in and bought Ragan what was most likely his last milkshake.

Jones' kindness eventually paid off. A few days later Ragan asked to speak to Chief Jones,

> Ragan said, "It came down just like you had it put together. I trust you. I won't talk to anyone but you. There are some things I could clear up if I knew I wouldn't get prosecuted for it. I could clear the board some."

In an extremely controversial move, Chief Jones spoke to prosecutors and asked to grant immunity for Ragan from any prosecution for crimes other than homicide or crimes out of his jurisdiction. The prosecution agreed.

Ragan then admitted to setting the Lemac Apartments on fire. On the evening of January 5, just before midnight, Ragan was parked near the building.

> "It was so ugly. I just went back to burn it down because it was ugly."

He told police that he was drunk and simply wedged newspaper into the frame of the building and lit it ablaze. He also admitted to setting several other fires in the area including forest fires, buildings and bridges—with no regard for human life. He said he always just used newspapers and a match.

He then confessed to several other burglaries, larcenies, assaults and another rape of a young boy.

Ragan was found guilty of second degree murder, being a habitual criminal, second degree assault with a deadly weapon in the first degree, and two counts of sodomy.

In an unprecedented move the prosecutor tried him for a second habitual criminal charge strictly to solidify the chance that he would never be released.

> "Under our present system of perpetual appeals and post-conviction writs, no condition is 100 percent solid."

Tommy Ragan was convicted of a total of seven felonies in Washington and another burglary conviction in Alaska. As of this writing, seventy-seven-year-old Ragan is still held in the Monroe Correctional Complex in Monroe, Washington. His listed possible release date is July 17, 2022.

CHAPTER 3
THE BODY IN THE BAG

A s a young child in suburban Sydney, Australia, Will Matheson seemed to be a normal kid by all accounts. But life at home was far from normal. Will was born in 1982 to two talented and highly intelligent parents, but their eccentricities were beyond extreme.

His mother was a professional violinist and his father was a former teacher and musician who collected junk for a hobby. As a young boy Will and his father would walk the streets late at night rummaging through garbage cans and dumpsters looking for anything his father might find interesting.

The Matheson family were extreme hoarders. Their home was in constant disarray, filled to the ceiling with a chaotic mess of junk, leaving only a small path to walk between rooms. Will's parents didn't have a bedroom, instead they pulled out a small mattress and laid it on the kitchen floor every night.

Both his mother and father suffered from psychiatric problems and his older brother, Edward, had been diagnosed with schizophrenia.

Will was just nine years old when his seventeen-year-old brother was admitted to a mental hospital. During a visit by Will, he and Edward walked the grounds of the institution. Edward led Will to the roof of the building where he jumped to his death while Will watched in horror.

At such a young age, Will was unable to properly process what had happened and his eccentric parents weren't best suited to help him. Will retreated into his mind and his own eccentricities. By his teenage years Will had developed a deep fixation with death. He listened to music called Horrorcore, a subgenre of Rap music, but with psychotic, supernatural, and violent themes.

Though Will didn't have many friends, he became known throughout the school as "PK", an acronym for "Porn King", because he would duplicate porn tapes and sell them to the boys in his school.

Like his family members, Will excelled musically. He played several instruments, but was a particularly talented cellist, playing in a quartet that would often play gigs at various events.

When he finished high school in 2000, Will had no close friends to speak of apart from the friends in his quartet. Like his father, he scavenged things from the streets of Sydney and developed a fascination with dead animals. His bedroom was decorated with his collection of bones, skulls, and dead animal skins he had collected.

Will made a living breeding rats. His bedroom and bathroom were filled with as many as 300 rats, some in cages, some running loose.

After graduation from high school, Will remained in his quartet and occasionally played paid gigs. It was at one of these gigs in April 2001, a wedding, that he met Lyndsay Van Blanken.

———

Eighteen-year-old Will Matheson was a last-minute replacement for the regular cellist in the quartet, and fifteen-year-old Lyndsay was a bridesmaid at her mother's wedding. Lyndsay's best friend noticed Matheson and by the end of the evening gave him both her own number and Lyndsay's.

Lyndsay Van Blanken was like any other young Australian girl. She was shy, loved to play online video games, and had a passion for drawing. She dreamed of working in animation someday.

Not long after the wedding, Lyndsay and Will began dating, but it was an odd relationship. Will was aloof and non-committal, always keeping her at arm's length. Perhaps this intrigued her, or perhaps she was fascinated by his dark side.

Over time, the two developed a relationship, and Lyndsay started to change. She became fascinated by the same macabre things as Will. She began to dress in dark drab clothes like him, talk like him, and would walk the streets at night with him, often through cemeteries. Though the two grew close, Will remained reserved and distant. He was Lyndsay's first boyfriend and his indifference only intrigued her more.

Eventually Will confided to her that his brother had committed suicide in front of him and he told her of his own suicidal thoughts. One evening when they were chatting on the computer he told her he was going to kill himself. Terrified, Lyndsay had her parents rush her to his house, but when she arrived in tears, he was laughing at her. He had been toying with her the whole time.

On Valentine's day she bought a small teddy bear and a single rose and placed it on the front steps of Will's home. When Lyndsay's mother later asked her how he liked the present, she told her mother that he gave it back to her. He told Lyndsay that he wasn't the sort of person that wanted presents. Their relationship was an unconventional one.

Lyndsay was a talented artist, having drawn since a very young age. The longer she dated Will, the more her drawings and paintings became sinister and eerie. By the time she turned sixteen, her parents began to worry about her new persona, and with good reason. Lyndsay had always been an excellent student, but uncharacteristically she became depressed and dropped out of school during her senior year.

After more than two years of dating, Lyndsay knew her relationship with Will was affecting her life negatively. She wanted to end it, but had no idea how to break it off.

Lyndsay loved to play online video games and used the nickname demon_nurse. One of her regular opponents in the online game was a twenty-year-old from Seattle named Brandon Leonard. After several months of playing online with Brandon, they began chatting and sending photos to each other. Though they hadn't met in person, it wasn't long before the exchange formed into an online romance.

Though Lyndsay was now committed to her online boyfriend Brandon, she still hadn't broken it off with Will. As with many eighteen-year-old girls, she just didn't know how to do it and kept putting it off.

During the same time, Lyndsay had heard that Disney Animation Studios had opened an office in Sydney and they were looking for trainee animation artists. It was her dream job. Lyndsay submitted her illustrations, as did over 300 other applicants. To her delight, Lyndsay was the most talented of the applicants and started her exciting new career with Disney.

Lyndsay's parents were elated. Her attitude toward every-thing began to change back to the old Lyndsay. She started dressing in more presentable clothes, went back to her cheerful attitude and saw Will less and less.

Brandon was happy for her as well and the two of them were now madly in love. That's when Brandon proposed to her over the internet and she joyfully accepted.

On September 8, 2003, Lyndsay knew it was time to break it off with Will. Brandon was flying to Sydney the next day, and she knew it had to be done. When she told Will it was over, he was heartbroken and angry. He cried, pled with her, and told her he would kill himself, but she was steadfast and ended their relationship. However, she didn't tell him about Brandon, or that they were planning to get married.

When Brandon arrived in Sydney the two of them were a happy couple planning the rest of their lives together, but Will had no intention of letting her go. He began stalking her on her way to work at her new job.

When Will inevitably saw Lyndsay with Brandon, he exploded in anger. Knowing he could never get Lyndsay back, he confronted Brandon at the apartment where he was staying.

Will told the few friends he had that he was considering suicide. He was still deeply in love with Lyndsay, but he hated her at the same time. His anger consumed him.

Lyndsay was terrified. Will spent almost every day following her to and from work. He would be waiting at bus stops knowing the times she was due to show up. He would even stand across the street in the middle of the night, staring up at her bedroom window. This went on for two months. He wanted her to know he would be a part of her life whether she liked it or not.

Brandon wanted Lyndsay to meet his parents and the two of them made plans to travel back to Seattle for Christmas. On November 22, Lyndsay got a text from Matheson. "I see you," was all it said. Terrified, she broke down crying. Her parents reassured her and told her not to worry, she would leave for Seattle soon and it would all be over.

On November 24, one of Lyndsay's coworkers at Disney noticed her arguing with a young man outside of the office during the lunch break. He could see it was a heated argument, but didn't want to interfere. That same evening Lyndsay took the train back to her home in Queen's Park. She got off the train at the Bondi Junction railway station where she was seen on security cameras at 5:58 p.m. leaving the station. That would be the last time she was seen alive.

That evening when Lyndsay didn't arrive at home at her normal time, Brandon and her parents became worried. Though they tried all night long, there was no answer from her phone and no text messages. Early the next morning Brandon called the police and reported his fiancé missing.

Her parents explained to the police that it was completely out of character for Lyndsay to disappear on her own. They also informed the police that she was being stalked by her ex-boyfriend, Will Matheson.

The family suspected Will had something to do with her disappearance, and Lyndsay's older sister Louise called Will to see what he had to say. Will claimed he had seen Lyndsay that evening as she got off the train at Bondi Junction. He told Louise that he had walked with her toward her home for about ten or fifteen minutes, then left her. He said that the last time he saw her was in an alley behind the Charing Cross Pub. Louise thought it was odd that Lyndsay would be in an alley behind a pub. Walking through an alley was not something that Lyndsay would normally do.

Adding more confusion to the call, Will's eccentric father burst in on the line during their conversation and said,

"Well, I didn't see any blood on his hands."

This startled Louise, and she later informed police about the strange conversation.

Two days after she had gone missing, the police pulled Matheson into the station for an interview. He was calm and morose, speaking in a monotone. His demeanor alone raised the police's suspicion. Again, Matheson stuck to his story and said that he had walked with her after she had got off of the train, then left her.

Investigators asked for a DNA swab, fingerprints, and photographs, and Matheson agreed. But when he pulled off his shirt for the photographs, it raised hairs on the back of investigator's necks. He had several cuts and scrapes on his chest, hands, and arms. He also had scrapes on his knees.

Will explained that the cuts and scrapes were from his rats and cats, and he claimed the scrapes on his knees were from a skateboarding fall.

Matheson told the police that when he heard Lyndsay was missing, he called her family and her friends. But the police noticed something he had omitted. He didn't mention that he had actually tried to call Lyndsay. If he believed she was still alive, he would have tried to call her. This was yet another aspect of the interview that raised the police's suspicion; they were sure he was involved. But with no definitive evidence, they had to let him go.

Detectives retraced her last steps, and an extensive search of the area began. Police searched parks and streets in the area and divers searched the lakes in Centennial Park near her home, but their efforts garnered no clues.

Police then showed Lyndsay's coworker a line-up of mugshots to see if he recognized the person that was arguing with Lyndsay outside of her office that day. He easily pointed out Will Matheson.

Two weeks after Lyndsay's disappearance, police received a phone call at 1:30 a.m. from a member of the public reporting what they thought was a prowler. When the police arrived, they found Will Matheson walking the streets and alleys carrying a backpack. Inside that backpack was another backpack containing several suspicious items: A pair of metal scissors, a box cutter, and a hatchet. They also found three pairs of latex surgical gloves, hospital grade disinfectant, two flashlights, candles and candleholders, black plastic garbage bags, several newspapers, moisturizer, and a small bottle of water. Matheson told police it was "holy water."

Police brought Matheson in for questioning, and again his demeanor was subdued. He claimed the items were for "a picnic."

> Investigator: "What can you tell me about those items?"
>
> Matheson: "I was going to um… go up to the park and have a… picnic."
>
> Investigator: "At 1:30 in the morning?"
>
> Matheson: "Yeah."

Police suspected Lyndsay was already dead and his plans were to dismember and dispose of her body. Again, they had no definitive evidence that they could use to hold him. Matheson was free to go, but police started twenty-four-hour surveillance on him.

———

On January 10, 2004, the residents of a small apartment building in Queen's Park complained to their building maintenance man of a horrible stench coming from the storage room below the apartments.

The maintenance man went into the storage room and noticed a mattress covering an interior doorway. When he pulled the mattress away and pushed the door open a horrid smell knocked him back. The small room was filled with junk, boxes, and furniture. As he pushed aside items and made his way to the back of the room, he noticed an over-sized sports bag. It was a huge bag used to carry cricket bats and equipment. He tried to pick it up, but couldn't. It was too heavy. Barely able to handle the foul smell, he dragged the bag out of the room into the open air. He then used a pock-etknife to cut it open and a small human hand fell out.

When detectives arrived, they had a sinking feeling it was the body of Lyndsay Van Blanken. Before they had a chance to identify her, the media got word of the body being found and broadcast it on the news. Lyndsay's grandmother saw the news and called her granddaughter Louise and asked if it might be Lyndsay. Louise assured her grandmother that if it was Lyndsay, the police would surely have alerted the family before they would let the media know.

Louise's curiosity overwhelmed her and she called the lead investigator. Sadly, the investigator told her that it might be the body of Lyndsay. Using the clothes she was wearing and the engagement ring on her finger, they positively identified her as Lyndsay Van Blanken.

She had been strangled using cable ties. Two cable ties had been put together to make a loop large enough to slip over her head and a quick pull would have ratcheted down on her throat. The loop had been tightened down to only ten inches, closing off her ability to breathe. Her fingernails were almost ripped off, most likely from scratching her attacker. Her body had then been folded and stuffed into the bag, then tucked in the corner of the storage room for eight weeks.

The day after Lyndsay's body was found Will Matheson was having a mental breakdown. He told his father he was hearing voices in his head. Will sat his father down in front of the television and showed him the nightly news he had recorded of Lyndsay's body being found. His parents called the hospital and mental health workers admitted him into a psychiatric hospital where he remained for the next eight weeks.

Will's father said, "So he came inside and looked at the midnight news. And when he finished looking at it he just sat down and cried. He said 'I think I've done that.' And he pulled his legs into his chest in the fetal position and just cried and cried."

Because Will had been admitted to a mental hospital, police were not able to question him, but they were allowed to search the family home.

Inside Will's bedroom was a stench almost as bad as a rotting corpse, but the smell came from his rats and rat excrement. There were rats everywhere, and the ceiling was covered with flies. Will had collected clippings from all the newspapers with any stories pertaining to Lyndsay. The room was full of keepsakes of Lyndsay such as notes, letters, and videotapes. Also in his room was Lyndsay's diary of notes and drawings. It was a very personal and precious diary to her that she would never have given to Will or anyone else. The most incriminating evidence was found in the top drawer of his dresser. They found a small Dictaphone and two tapes.

When police played the tapes, they found what they considered to be a confession. One tape had a song he had recorded in a muted, tragic voice. The lyrics were:

"Just the other day I watched you pass away. You said I love you. Please let me stay. Help is not here for you or me. Close your eyes. When you go is where I'll be. I'll meet you in eternity."

He also spoke in a whispering voice into the Dictaphone,

"It's all because of him. He didn't want you to hurt me as a friend. I hope you understand that. I didn't want to let you go. I told you I didn't want to let you go."

In many of the additional musings on the tapes he spoke of Lyndsay in the past-tense.

When detectives questioned his parents, Will's father admitted that he had been shopping with his son in Bondi Junction two days before Lyndsay went missing. He told police that when Will returned to the car, he was carrying a large sports bag.

The bag that Lyndsay's body was found in was a very specific type of cricket bag. Using the brand and model of the bag, police were able to find that there was only one store in the area which carried that specific bag, and they had only sold one of them. It was sold two days before Lyndsay went missing at 1:30 p.m. for $120 and was paid for in cash.

Investigators then searched through security cameras in the Bondi Junction shopping area during the time that Will's father said the two of them were there. They found footage of Will walking near Rebel Sports just before 1:30 p.m.

In March 2004 Will Matheson was discharged from the psychiatric hospital and police immediately brought him back in for additional questioning.

Despite his admission to his father and to hospital staff, during his interrogation he continued to deny any involvement in Lyndsay's death. Even when shown the video evidence, Matheson still denied purchasing the sports bag.

Detectives then took Matheson on a walk around Bondi Junction and ended up at the storage room where her body was found. He admitted he and Lyndsay had been in the storage room months before, but claimed he had never been into the interior room. When they asked him to walk into the interior room and told him that was where her body was found he broke down and asked to leave,

> "Can we go somewhere else. Can we just go somewhere else."

Again, without sufficient grounds, the police let him go while they gathered more evidence. Surprisingly, just a few days later, Matheson requested another interview with the police. He had something to tell them.

In the subsequent interview Matheson confided that he had been hearing voices,

> Matheson: "I've been under distress of mental problems, hearing voices and the such."
>
> Police: "What are these voices saying to you?"
>
> Matheson: "Just... to cause destruction. To kill people. To cause harm to myself."

Despite having no previous diagnosis, Matheson and his parents claimed he was mentally ill.

On May 19, 2004, police arrested Will Matheson for the murder of Lyndsay Van Blanken.

The prosecution spent the next year and a half preparing for the trial. During the trial Matheson was as emotionless as ever and had trouble maintaining eye contact with anyone in the courtroom.

Despite his claims of mental illness, the prosecution showed that the murder was premeditated. He had purchased the cricket bag just two days prior to killing her; he had tied two cable-ties together and trimmed off the edges making it easier to slip over her head. He had lured her to the store-room and had the bag there waiting for her. All the evidence showed that he had clearly planned the murder ahead of time. The judge found that whatever psychiatric condition he had been suffering from had little to do with his premeditation.

In 2006 Will Matheson was sentenced to a minimum of eighteen years in prison without the chance of parole, and a maximum of twenty-seven years. In 2015, however, the court ruled that a legal error had been made during his trial and his maximum sentence was reduced, making him eligible for parole in 2022. Though he had originally denied his involvement in her murder, once in prison he finally admitted that he had killed Lyndsay.

————

In 2016 a backpack was found when a construction crew was clearing a building site in the Sydney suburb of Randwick. The backpack was determined to belong to Lyndsay Van Blanken, and inside they found over forty bone fragments. Twelve of the bones were human, and the remainder were from animals. Of the human bones, one was a leg bone, and another was a skull fragment with a nail driven through it. The bones belonged to as many as eleven different humans.

Forensic pathologists, however, determined that the bones were most likely just random bones from medical cadavers that Matheson had collected for his collection and were not connected to a murder.

CHAPTER 4
MR. MOM KILLER

I n 2007, Washington International Group was a successful multi-billion dollar company that provided engineering and construction services in more than thirty countries around the world. Tara Grant was a successful, well-educated, and well-paid executive in the company. Though she was a systems manager based in the Detroit, Michigan office, she commuted Monday through Friday all over the world. Every Friday evening she would hop back on a plane so she could spend the weekends with her two young children and husband, Stephen Grant.

On Valentine's Day 2007 Stephen walked into the Macomb County Sheriff's office to report his wife missing.

———

Tara Destrampe grew up in a tiny town called Perkins with a population of less than 100 located in the upper peninsula of Michigan. Though the rest of her family was perfectly happy with small-town life, Tara was destined for more. Even from a young age she wanted to excel in her life and longed for the big city life. She was determined to go out into the world and create her fortune.

In her teenage years Tara grew into a brash, outspoken young woman, often berating and verbally attacking boyfriends who didn't seem strong enough in her eyes. She was known for her controlling nature and her explosive anger.

After graduating third in her high school class, Tara attended Michigan State University in Lansing. It was there that she first met Stephen Grant.

During the Summer of 1994, Tara was just finishing up her degree. Stephen was in her immediate group of friends and had pursued Tara for several months before she finally gave in and accepted his invitation for a date.

Stephen was obnoxious and a bit awkward, but he wasn't submissive like other boys that Tara had dated. She saw potential in him. Though he had dropped out of college, he worked in the office of a Michigan State Senator and that impressed her. Steven often bragged of his aspirations to pursue a law degree and she envisioned him having a career in politics.

Stephen knew that Tara had grown up in a tiny town and longed for the big city life. On their first date he gave her a tour of Detroit, driving her through the mansions of Gross Pointe, the Detroit Institute of Arts, and taking her for a meal in Greek Town. Tara was impressed, but what really sealed the deal for her was when her grandmother died, Stephen showed up unannounced to the funeral to console her and charmed her family. Tara was in love.

That December Tara graduated from university and moved in with Steven. It wasn't long after that before he proposed, and she cheerfully accepted.

Eventually Stephen's job with the senator ended, and he was perpetually having trouble finding work. In early 1995 Steven's father offered him a job at the family tool and die shop in Mount Clemens, just north of Detroit. The pay wasn't that great, but it was enough to survive and Tara liked that it was closer to a big city.

In September 1996 Tara and Stephen were married and Tara got a temporary job at a company called Morrison Knudsen which would later be acquired by Washington International Group. She was a perfect fit for the company and was very focused on her new career. It wasn't long before her determination paid off and she was quickly offered a permanent position.

Though money was still tight, the couple had their first child, a daughter, in 2000. Two years later they had a son. Even through the pregnancies, Tara continued climbing the corporate ladder, eventually landing a high-paying executive job. By 2003 her job duties required her to travel to sites where the company had construction jobs all over the globe, which left Stephen to deal with the children.

Stephen, still working at the tool and die shop, couldn't work and take care of the kids, so the couple hired an au pair. Through the years the Grants went through seven different au pairs, eventually settling on a beautiful nineteen-year-old from Germany, Verena Dierke.

Stephen spent as much time as he could with the kids, but because of her job, Tara was only able to squeeze in the weekends. Though the income she brought in was good,

Stephen resented his wife for leading a jet-setter lifestyle while he stayed at home.

By 2006 Tara was making $168,000 a year. Even her year-end bonus of $28,000 was more than the measly $19,000 he was bringing home from his father's machine shop.

As an executive, Tara was on a regular schedule of flying Monday through Friday 2,000 miles away to San Juan, Puerto Rico. The flight was five hours each way, but she came home to be with the family every weekend.

Over time, Steven's resentment of Tara continued to build. But when Tara decided to start taking golf lessons on the weekend, it didn't sit well with Stephen. Tara, always wanting to enhance her career, knew that lots of business took place on the golf course.

Frustrated and angry with the lack of attention from his wife, Stephen developed a relationship with their young au pair, Verena. It started out as harmless flirting, but in early February 2007 it became physical. It started with kissing and continued with him requesting sex. On Thursday, February 8, before Tara returned home from Puerto Rico, he gave her oral sex for the first time.

While Tara was in San Juan that week she wrote a lengthy letter to Stephen. In the letter she apologized to him for pushing him away and making him feel inadequate. She thought it would be a good idea for them to renew their wedding vows. Tara possibly intended to give him the letter on Valentine's Day the following week, but she never got the chance. By Valentine's Day Stephen had walked into the Macomb County sheriff's department and reported his wife missing.

As Stephen talked to detectives, he gave a long and rambling description of what had happened five days prior; the night she went missing. He said that he and Tara argued that Friday night over the phone as she drove home from the airport. She had been delayed by a snowstorm and informed him she would need to go right back to San Juan the next day.

When she got home, they argued for twenty minutes more before she made a phone call and told someone to come pick her up. He assumed she had called the car service she normally used to take her to the airport. Stephen told detectives the last thing she said to him was to make sure to bring the car to the dealership on Monday to get a dent fixed. Then a black car came to the front of the house, she got into the back, and it drove away. Ten minutes later their au pair, Verena, came home.

When detectives asked why Stephen had waited so long to report his wife missing, he told them it was the suggestion of her boss. Stephen had called her work just after she went missing and her boss told him he knew nothing about Tara needing to go back to San Juan early, but advised him to wait before reporting her missing and he would talk to public relations first. Stephen had also called Tara's sister and mother, but neither of them had heard from her. He told them he'd be happy to know she was just in a hotel with a lover. He just wanted to make sure she was ok.

Stephen told the police he didn't trust Tara's mother or her boss and suspected they were both lying to him—possibly trying to cover up an affair she was having with her boss. Stephen then confided to the police that he and Tara had been to marriage counseling and he was considering hiring a divorce lawyer. To detectives, this was an immediate red flag.

Stephen then rambled on about the company that she worked for. He explained that Washington International Group was involved in the manufacture of chemical weapons and suggested possibly that she had been exposed to nerve gas or kidnapped by terrorists. Again, detectives thought these were extremely odd details to add to the story.

During the questioning, in an attempt to show detectives he was honest, Stephen also admitted that he had a warrant out for his arrest for unpaid traffic tickets. Detectives weren't interested in that and let him go and started their investigation.

When asked about their au pair, Verena, and if he was having a relationship with her, Stephen jokingly replied, "she'll never tell," and left it at that. What he didn't tell the police was that he and Verena had had sex for the first time just minutes after he claimed Tara disappeared in the black car.

The interviewing officer also took note of a scratch on Stephen's nose and asked if he had got into a fight with Tara on the night she left. Stephen said he hadn't, but he said that he told her if she went back to Puerto Rico the kids wouldn't even miss her because he was the one that took them to soccer every day.

Then he told the detective he wasn't even sure if he wanted Tara to come back, and that his family all thought she was having an affair with her boss.

The first thing detectives did after Stephen left was to call Tara's work. Her boss confirmed that she hadn't shown up for work that week and had never missed a day of work in her ten years with the company. Tara also used a company cell phone and credit card. Her employer verified that neither had been used since she had arrived home the evening of February 9.

The police also contacted Tara's family. Her sister told them that she had spoken to Tara for forty minutes during her layover in Newark on February 9 and she hadn't mentioned anything about going back to Puerto Rico early that weekend.

Police were instantly suspicious of Stephen and assigned someone to watch his house, but Stephen wasn't stupid and noticed right away. When he called the lead investigator to complain, the investigator explained that they couldn't be too careful and asked if he could come over to Stephen's and ask him a few more questions.

When Detective Sergeant Brian Kozlowski arrived at the Grant house, he brought Detective Sgt. Pamela McLean with him. Kozlowski took Stephen into the kitchen to question him more while McLean questioned Verena.

Verena told Detective McLean that she was out with some friends on the Friday evening and when she arrived home that night Tara had already gone and the kids were asleep. She told the detective that she thought it was odd that Tara had left and that she had called a car service to take her to the airport. She told police that Tara normally drove herself to the airport each week. This contradicted what Stephen had told the police. He told them Tara had always used a car service.

In the kitchen, Detective Kozlowski asked Stephen about the scratch on his nose. Stephen claimed he had received the scratch while working at the machine shop. He said that some metal shavings had got under his safety goggles, and then showed Kozlowski scratches and bruises on his hands and legs, claiming they were all from his work.

Kozlowski then asked if Stephen had been having an affair. He denied it; he said that Tara had had an affair in the past, but it was now over.

The detectives then asked if they could search the house and Stephen agreed. Inside they found a handgun with two loaded magazines and some duct tape in the master bedroom. Stephen told them he had just forgotten to put away the gun.

On the master bedroom nightstand they found a red photo journal that belonged to Verena. This struck detectives as odd because the journal was in the master bedroom and not in Verena's own bedroom.

When detectives checked the walk-in closet, they noticed there were no empty spaces where Tara kept all of her business suits. Her suitcase was still in the closet, but Stephen explained that she had packed a second suitcase for the trip.

The following day Stephen was pulled over and arrested for driving on a suspended license. Stephen complained that the police were just using that as an excuse to detain him. After the arrest police searched his car and found two envelopes of cash totaling $3,000.

Stephen immediately hired the most expensive attorney in town and was released on bail within six hours. From that point forward Stephen was much more cautious. He refused to answer any questions without his attorney present, and only in writing.

Stephen had no problem talking to the media though. He loved to cry in front of the cameras, pleading for the safe return of his wife. He naturally had strange facial expressions and bulging eyes, which only made his crying seem more awkward and forced. Initially, his appearances were filled with tears, but over time the tears dried up and he began complaining about her excessive business travel and the possibility that she was having an affair.

> "I get that she has to travel for business, but too much is too much, and that was too much."

> "A couple of years ago, Tara and I did have a problem in our marriage with the… I don't want to call it an infidelity, but pretty close to an infidelity."

The denigration of his wife didn't play well with the local TV viewers who began to question his sincerity.

The police asked Stephen to take a polygraph, but he denied their request. Instead he and his attorney opted to have him take a polygraph privately, but police assumed he must have failed the test as Stephen kept the results to himself.

Having seen Stephen on the nightly news, a former girlfriend of his came forward and told police she had recently received emails from him which read,

> "I am still in need of some excitement in my day ... Wink wink! I just think of marriage vows like speed limits. Sometimes you have to break them."

As police looked further into Stephen's explanation of Tara's disappearance they came across more and more holes in the story. Airline records showed no flights with Tara on them and her normal flight booking for the following Monday had gone unused.

Her cell phone records also didn't show a call at the time that Stephen said she called a car service. The last call on her phone was to Stephen eighteen minutes before she had arrived home that night.

Despite Stephen claiming she always used a car service, she had actually only used a car service once in the past year. Police verified that she almost always drove herself to the airport and parked her car in the airport parking lot during the week. Additionally, nothing had been charged to her credit cards since she had paid for the airport parking at the lot that night on her way home.

Stephen's cell phone records, however, were much busier. That evening he had called Verena four times. In the days following her disappearance Stephen had called Tara's phone six times pleading for her to come home.

> "Hey, I get that you're pissed at me. I just left the house; I have to go to the bank for my dad. Verena's at the house with the kids. Please, at least call your kids. It's ridiculous Tara. It's not right. Just call please so I can talk to you. They didn't get to see you last night."

> "It's me. Call us. Just let us know what's going on. The kids and I would like to talk to you. Please. I just don't know what the deal is so call me. We're here. I'm just ordering pizza for dinner so we'll be here. I'm just gonna have it delivered I think, so call us. Bye."

In other messages he showed his anger,

> "Tara, next time I call you, pick up your phone. It's absolute bullshit that you can't call me or your kids. I know you're mad. I'm mad too. You traveling this much is not right."

During the initial interview Stephen had mentioned several times that he and Tara spent quite a bit of time exercising in nearby Stoney Creek Park. The police now suspected that Stephen had killed his wife and possibly dumped her body in the park. Eight days after her disappearance, police began an extensive search of the area.

Stoney Creek Park was over 4,000 acres of thick woods and swamps. The media carried the story of the search and Stephen spoke to the cameras several times, playing the role of grieving husband,

> "Please call anybody. Call the police, call me, call my in-laws, call someone."

On the afternoon of February 28, a woman was walking along Mt. Vernon Road on the edge of Stoney Creek Park, not far from the Grants' home. Just a few yards from the roadway she noticed something plastic crammed between the branches of a fallen tree. When she got closer, she could see that it was a large, one-gallon ziplock bag with something red inside. The red color stood out in stark contrast to the snowy surroundings. When she picked up the bag she could see that the red was from blood pooling in the bottom of the bag.

Inside the bag, police found four clear plastic garbage bags, one pair of latex gloves, metal shavings, a 7-11 bag and another ziplock bag. All the items were covered in human blood.

Using the newly found evidence, detectives were able to get two search warrants: One for Stephen Grant's home and another for his father's tool and die shop.

When police broke the door down at the tool and die shop, they found a dark and messy metal shop. Metal lathes, presses and other work equipment were covered with thick metal dust. What stood out to investigators was a large, clean, square-shaped area on the floor. It looked as if someone had laid a tarp there. On the floor directly under the door handle they found what seemed to be a few tiny drops of blood.

Simultaneously, another group of police showed up at the Grants' house. Though Stephen wasn't home, live news cameras filmed as officers entered the house. When Stephen arrived home shortly after the police had entered, they stopped his car as he drove up the street. Police requested him not to disturb the search and he was calm and cooperative, but asked officers if he could take his dog for a walk. Police agreed and Stephen put a leash on his dog and walked down the snowy streets while television cameras watched him leave.

As investigators searched the house, they noticed a green Rubbermaid tub with a blue lid in the garage next to a little red wagon full of children's toys.

Detective Kozlowski pulled off the lid to the tub and found a pile of black plastic bags stacked near the top. He touched the top one and noticed it was soft and mushy. As he tugged at the black bags, it tore and showed another bag and another bag. As he got deeper, he came to a clear plastic bag smeared with blood.

Using a flashlight, Kozlowski initially thought possibly Stephen was storing some deer meat in the freezing cold garage, but as he dug deeper, he found a woman's bra. It was clear this was the body of Tara Grant.

The tub was filled with Tara's frozen torso. The arms were severed at the shoulders, and the legs were severed at the tops of the thighs. Her head, arms, and legs were all missing. The torso still wore the gray Ann Taylor blouse that Stephen had told police she was wearing when she disappeared.

Investigators now realized that Stephen had been walking the dog for more than an hour and hadn't returned to the house. He was on the run, and the manhunt began.

Stephen, of course, knew exactly what the police would find. When he left the house with his dog, he phoned his friend Mike Zanlungo, a neighbor in the same subdivision. Stephen told Mike that he needed to borrow his truck for a bit so he could go visit his children at his sister's house. Mike later said that trusting him was the biggest mistake of his life.

Stephen took Mike's truck and headed towards his sister Kelly's house. He called his sister as he drove; she told him they weren't at home, but were at their church having a fish fry.

Stephen drove to the church and met his sister in the hallway. She immediately noticed he was extremely agitated and disoriented. He told Kelly,

> "I'm going to get arrested. They told me if they find a drop of blood in my house I'm going to prison."

Stephen then kissed his kids goodbye and drove to his sister's house to drop off the dog. When he got to the house, he looked for her .38 handgun, but couldn't find it. Instead, he grabbed a full bottle of Vicodin that he found in the medicine cabinet and got back in the truck.

He drove toward Lansing, Michigan drinking whiskey and taking Vicodin the whole way. Along the route he stopped to buy razor blades, a pre-paid burner phone, a notebook, Tylenol PM, a black Sharpie pen and a plastic toy gun. He was intent on killing himself, but was worried that he wouldn't have the nerve to do it himself. He took the Sharpie pen and marked over the red end-cap of the toy gun. He hoped that if the police found him, he could pull the gun on them and they would shoot and kill him.

As he drove Stephen avoided highways and took the back roads. He stopped again to get $500 out of an ATM and bought more whiskey and some Baileys Irish Cream.

Highly intoxicated and crying, Stephen called his sister one last time and called Verena, who was now in Germany. At 1:30 a.m. he made one last call to his attorney who encouraged him not to kill himself and to come back home, telling him that his kids needed him.

Stephen cried,

> "She treated us like shit. It's her fault this happened. Everyone hates me, but it's her fault. She cheated on me, she left us alone, we meant nothing to her. Tell my kids I love them. I tried to be a good dad. I did. I love them so damn much."

At 3:30 a.m. Stephen called his attorney again, telling him it was all an accident and the only way out of it was if he ended his own life.

Barely able to speak from the drugs and alcohol, Stephen again called Verena and then called his sister Kelly one last time. He told Kelly he was in the Wilderness State Park and was planning on killing himself. Police were already waiting outside her home. After the call she walked outside and told officers where to find him.

Detective Kozlowski's phone rang and when he saw that it was an international number he knew it was Verena Dierkes calling from Germany. Verena was crying and had just gotten off the phone with Stephen,

> "Everything he said was a lie. Everything. And I believed everything."

> "He told me it was an accident. He said, 'She smacked me and she yelled at me and I pushed her back and she banged her head and was dead.'"

Initially Verena denied having an affair with Stephen, but eventually admitted that it was true,

> "We liked each other. We liked each other more than we should. And it started about four weeks ago. It was just talking. I don't know what… maybe because Tara was always gone. And then… it just happened. But it was never physical. On that, I swear. We kissed, but that's all."

Detective Kozlowski questioned her more and got her to admit that Stephen had performed oral sex on her,

> "But it was just one time. And it was before that happened to Tara. It was before the… February the 9th."

Verena then told the detective that Stephen intended to kill himself.

Helicopters scoured the vast Wilderness State Park and quickly found his abandoned truck. Within a few hours searchers followed footsteps leading away from the truck and found his plastic gun, the notebook, and a half empty bottle of whiskey.

By 7:00 a.m. searchers found Stephen barely conscious in the snow beneath a tree. His body temperature was down to 78 degrees Fahrenheit. Suffering from severe hypothermia and frostbite, Stephen was airlifted to the nearest hospital.

That morning police searched Stoney Creek Park again. This time they found one of Tara's hands, her feet, a leg, and chunks of her flesh. Still in intensive care, Stephen was charged with murder and handcuffed to his hospital bed.

Though still suffering from hypothermia, Stephen just couldn't keep his mouth shut. His attorney had dropped him as a client; Stephen called Detective Kozlowski and told him he wanted to talk. When confronted with the evidence against him, he rambled on for almost four hours in a long detailed confession from his hospital bed.

He explained that Tara had come home that night, and they continued the argument that had started on the phone. He said that during their eleven-year marriage, Tara had constantly belittled him and he had had enough of it. When she slapped him in their bedroom, his anger grew out of control. He said he had told Verena that when he hit her, she fell and hit her head, but that was a lie. He had actually strangled her to death on the bedroom floor.

> Grant: "I was ready to go to bed, and it just kept getting worse and worse. And when she smacked me, I lost it. ... Tara had, as long as I can remember, she belittled me and - and her one way - she knew if she hit me I'd hit her back."

Grant: "She said, 'I got to do what I have to do in my job and it's none of your business.' So she started to turn around, and I grabbed her wrist ... 'Just stop,' I said, 'you're not going anywhere.' And I said, 'We're going to finish this conversation' and she slapped me ... and after that I don't really remember what happened ... she fell. I know that she banged the back of her head on the floor, and then she said something like, 'That's it. I'm going to take the kids. You're going to be fucking homeless. You're a piece of shit.' And I choked her on the carpet. She had started to get back up when I put my hand on her neck. I grabbed her neck and choked her."

Detective McLean: "Were you looking at her face?"

Grant: "No, I covered her face up."

Detective McLean: "What'd you cover her face up with?"

Grant: "Gray underwear or a gray t-shirt."

Detective Kozlowski: "How did you know that she had died?"

Grant: "When she stopped moving. And I was worried. I was really worried."

The Grants' children were asleep in their rooms down the hall while Stephen murdered their mother. Immediately after strangling his wife, Stephen sent a text to Verena, "You owe me a kiss." He left a note saying the same thing on her pillow, then returned to his dead wife on the bedroom floor.

Grant tied one of his belts around her neck and dragged her down the stairs and into the garage. He put her body in the back of her Isuzu Trooper SUV.

"And I dropped her. She was too hard to pick up, and the belt broke, and she fell. It was the most disgusting noise. It just sounded like dropping a watermelon on the cement."

Moments later Verena returned home,

"And I kept thinking we've got a body in this garage. What the hell do I do with the body? And thinking I killed my wife. I was thinking my life was over."

Stephen explained to detectives that he let the body sit in the back of the SUV all of that Saturday. On Sunday he drove her body to his father's tool and die shop, where he used the tools there to dismember her.

"So I looked around the shop ... I was looking for something. I was looking for a hacksaw or something."

"At some point I threw up. And I threw up again. And then I drank some more whiskey. And then I just told myself, 'look if you don't do this you're going to prison for the rest of your life.' ... and I kept cutting her up."

Worried that the body would smell, he put the body parts back into the SUV and came home to spend the rest of the day with Verena and the kids.

"I tried to make things as normal as possible for everybody. And I continuously flirted with Verena because I thought that was the only way I was going to be able to get through this."

That Sunday evening Stephen put the kids' red sled in the back of the SUV and at 3:00 a.m. he snuck out of the house and drove to Stony Creek Park to dispose of the body parts.

At the park he piled the body parts onto the sled and dragged it up a hill, but things went wrong,

> "And as soon as I started going it was like Keystone Cops. The sled took off and now I'm chasing after this sled that has my wife's cut-up body in it down a hill... finally got it stopped when it fell over and it broke. So now all these pieces are now fallen all over the place."

> "So Tara's torso I took, and I buried in the snow. And then the pieces I put on the sled and I buried that in the snow."

> "I'd done a very, very bad job of hiding anything. It's right there in the open."

By Tuesday evening he was worried that he had done a poor job of hiding the body parts and returned to the park. He cut open the clear plastic bags that he had wrapped the pieces in and distributed the parts randomly throughout the park, leaving one ziplock bag near the road that was later found.

The following week when Stephen heard that the police were going to search the park, he went back to gather the pieces.

> "I thought, I'm screwed. They're going to find that, because that torso at this point is still buried in the snow. I had to dig it out. It was frozen in the ground. I threw it over my shoulder and carried it."

Confused and worried that he would get caught, Stephen moved the body parts back and forth several times, eventually storing the torso in his garage.

And I kept thinking, 'I got away with this. I can't believe I got away with this.'

Search teams found other parts of Tara in the area where the first ziplock bag was discovered. Stephen had cut her body into fourteen different pieces, but some parts were never recovered. It was assumed that animals may have made off with the missing parts.

Despite his recorded confession, which Stephen also wrote and signed, he pleaded not guilty.

Verena, who had returned to Germany, came back for the trial to testify against Stephen. She told the jury how her employer constantly tried to kiss her, exposed himself to her, and eventually, just moments after he killed his wife, had sex with her.

On Friday, December 21, 2007, the jury found Stephen Grant guilty of second degree murder and sentenced him to fifty years in prison. Stephen tried to appeal the decision, but was denied and will likely spend fifty to eighty years behind bars.

Tara's sister was given control of the estate, and custody of their two children, but their grandfather, Stephen's father, was denied visitation rights. Stephen's father tried desperately to regain visitation rights, but eventually lost hope and committed suicide in June 2008.

Tara's children now participate in a yearly walk called "Tara's Walk". The walk has raised tens of thousands of dollars to help the victims of domestic violence.

(The complete text of Stephen Grant's confession is available in the online appendix at the end of this book.)

CHAPTER 5
THE INCEST KILLER

Alyssa Garcia met twenty-year-old Steven Pladl in 1995 in an online chatroom when she was just fifteen years old. Alyssa lived in San Antonio, Texas, and Steven lived 2,000 miles away in New York. Alyssa would later recall that Steven was "grooming" her.

Within a year Alyssa had run away from home to be with Steven, married, and pregnant. By the age of just seventeen, she and Steven had a baby girl and named her Denise.

Shortly after the birth, Alyssa realized that Steven wasn't prepared for fatherhood. Beside the fact that they were poor and could barely afford to feed themselves, Steven had no patience with the child. When the baby cried he would put her in an empty ice chest and close the lid. When Alyssa saw Steven pinch Denise's arm just to see if he could make it turn black and blue, she knew what she needed to do.

Alyssa put baby Denise up for adoption. Eight-month-old Denise was adopted by a happy, loving family in Dover, New

York and spent the rest of her life with a new name; Katie Fusco.

> Alyssa later recalled, "It was so hard to give her up, but I had to because I wanted her to live and be happy."

––––––––

Despite the trauma of giving up her baby and having Steven's abuse directed at herself, Alyssa still stayed with him through the years. Though it was common for Steven to throw things around the house and punch holes in the drywall, she believed they were both "more grown up and ready." In 2007 they had another baby girl.

Steven's temper never ceased, but Alyssa still stayed in the relationship and in 2012 they had yet another baby girl. All the while, Alyssa was the subject of Steven's emotional and verbal abuse. By 2016 Steven and Alyssa were sleeping in separate rooms of the house and had decided they would separate later that year.

> "I was always on eggshells, whatever his mood was, everybody knew, and that mood was often not happy, a lot of yelling, a lot of things smashed in the house, in front of our kids."

––––––––

In January 2016 Tony and Kelly Fusco finally told their adopted daughter Katie that they were not her biological parents. Katie had just turned eighteen and like any adopted child, she grew curious about her biological parents.

In the years since Alyssa had given her up for adoption, Katie had led a normal American life. She had a brother and a sister, she was a vegetarian, loved animals and had the nickname "Pac-Man," because she was always eating.

Katie attended Dover High School, about eighty miles north of New York City, and loved to draw. She had plans to study digital advertising at the State University of New York, starting in August 2016.

> She wrote in a blog post, "A pen and something to draw on became a safe place for me. Ink became my weapon against rules and regulations. ... To be short; for me, a life without art is no life at all."

Katie's curiosity about her biological parents grew. It didn't take much to find Alyssa, now thirty-seven, and Steven Pladl, now forty-two, on social media and she messaged them. The couple, though on the verge of separation, happily invited her down to visit them in Henrico County, Virginia.

Katie's adoptive parents weren't happy about Katie visiting her biological parents, but believed she was eighteen and old enough to make her own decisions. Their apprehensions were confirmed, though, when Katie informed them that August that she had decided not to go to college and would move in with Alyssa and Steven instead.

Alyssa was also apprehensive. She was already on her way out of Steven's life when Katie moved in and privately informed Katie that the reason she gave her up for adoption was for her own safety. She told her of the abuse she had been subjected to when she was a baby, but Katie didn't seem to be concerned.

When Katie moved in with her biological parents, Steven's behavior changed. Suddenly he was wearing tight-fitting shirts, skinny jeans, shaved his beard and let his dark brown hair grow long.

Katie had been living with them less than two months when Steven spent the night on the floor in Katie's bedroom. When Steven did it again the following night Alyssa confronted him. He screamed at her, "It's none of your business!" then took Katie and left the house in a rage.

Steven's actions were more than Alyssa could take, and that November she separated from Steven, moved out of their house, and shared custody of their two other daughters. Katie remained living with Steven. Though she had no proof of it, Alyssa believed the relationship between Steven and Katie had gone too far.

In May 2017, Alyssa peeked inside her 11-year-old daughter's diary and saw what she had written about Katie. She was in for the shock of her life when she read,

> "… but now she is pregnant and gained weight and my dad calls her baby 'his' baby. Did he make her pregnant? My dad even says she's my 'stepmom.' WTF! He doesn't even want me to call her sister anymore. Katie is my sister. She's probably his wife now, but in nature she's only my sister. Does she see me as a daughter or a sister? Katie now tells me sometimes to 'get the fuck up!'"

Alyssa immediately called Steven,

> "I started to become hysterical, and I called him. I said, 'Is Katie pregnant with your baby?' He just said, 'I thought you knew. We're in love.' I started screaming. I was just

cursing him out: 'How could you? You're sick. She's a child.'"

Alyssa called the police, and an investigation began. Steven and Katie were interviewed by Henrico County police, as were the two other children, but no arrests were made. Steven and Alyssa's divorce was finalized days later.

Katie wore a short black dress and Steven wore a black shirt and black trousers at their July wedding in Maryland. Despite the investigation into their incestuous relationship, they lied on their marriage application and said they were not related. Steven's mother, Grace, was in attendance as were Katie's adoptive parents. Tony and Kelly Fusco believed that there was nothing they could do but show support for their daughter.

The couple had moved to Knightdale, North Carolina that summer and on September 1, 2017 Katie gave birth to a baby boy they named Bennett, but their family bliss wasn't destined to last long. In late November Henrico County police issued arrest warrants for both Steven and Katie Pladl.

In late January 2018 Steven and Katie were arrested in their Knightdale home and charged with incest and adultery, which was still a misdemeanor criminal offense in Virginia. Both were released on bond but ordered by the court to have no contact with one another.

Katie moved back to New York with her adoptive parents and custody of their four-month-old son Bennett was given to Steven's mother, Grace Pladl.

Steven's lawyer told the media that there was no accusation that Steven pressured Katie into the relationship, they were simply in love,

"This case is an eighteen-year-old girl who shows up at the doorstep of a forty-two-year-old man who's going through difficult times with his wife. They have a bond because they're biologically related, but they never knew each other before they had a sexual relationship. He was head over heels in love with her, so much so that that outweighed the issue of them being biologically related."

After spending the following two months with her adoptive parents in New York, Katie finally realized that her relationship with her biological father was wrong. Violating the no-contact order, Katie called Steven and gave him the news. Their relationship was over. Forever.

The news was more than Steven could handle. On April 11, 2018, Steven drove to his mother's house to pick up their baby boy. He took the seven-month-old Bennett back to his house, where he laid the boy on the floor and put a pillow over his face. Police later found the baby, suffocated and stuffed in a closet.

Immediately after killing their son, Steven drove nine hours through the night from North Carolina, north toward Katie.

Every Tuesday and Thursday Katie visited her adoptive grandmother in Waterbury, Connecticut. That morning Katie and her father Tony left their home in Dover for their trip to Waterbury while Steven watched from his minivan parked nearby.

Steven followed Katie and her father for fifteen miles before forcing them to the side of the road near New Milford, Connecticut. Steven jumped out of his van and pointed his AR-15 semi-automatic rifle at their truck and opened fire. Twenty-year-old Katie and her fifty-six-year-old father Tony

Fusco were both dead. Steven got back in his minivan and sped off.

An off-duty firefighter heard the shots and rushed to the scene just seconds after Steven had fled the scene. He called 911:

> "This is on Route 7 and 55. Someone just went by and shot this guy in the truck. I'm a firefighter out of New York. The car pulled up, went round and shot him. A whole clip full into his head. He's deceased, boss. The truck is in the middle of the road. He's dead. We need the police, we need everybody. There's two people in the car."

Steven called his mother as he drove toward Dover, New York. He told his mother that he had just killed Katie, her father, and their baby. Frantic, she hung up and called 911.

> "He left the baby dead. Oh God. He told me to call the police… I shouldn't go over there. The house is empty. He said he put a key under the front mat.

> His wife broke up with him yesterday over the phone. She's in New York and he told me he was on his way and after bringing the baby to her and then he was coming back. He killed his wife; he killed her father. I can't even believe this is happening."

Steven only drove nine miles back to Dover before he pulled over to the side of the road and killed himself with the same AR-15 rifle.

———

The case of Steven and Katie Pladl highlights a concept known as genetic sexual attraction. The term is used to describe a strong sexual attraction that develops between close relatives who meet for the first time as adults.

The concept is frequently reported as an unreliable anecdote and is often referred to as pseudoscience among psychology professionals since there have been no studies showing that people are attracted to people genetically similar to themselves.

CHAPTER 6
THE COPPER GULCH KILLER

I don't usually cover unsolved cases in the True Crime Case Histories series, but when I came across the story of the murder of Candace Hiltz it was just too engrossing to pass up. Though it's officially unsolved, there's plenty of suspicion and speculation.

————

Candace Hiltz was raised in the remote area of Copper Gulch, Colorado, an extremely rural area a few hours south of Denver. Though she was a small-town girl in every sense, she was exceedingly intelligent. By the age of eleven she was performing calculus, and by seventeen, when most of her friends were in high school, Candace was already in her third year of an online degree at Brigham Young University.

Candace dreamed of being a lawyer and was awarded a scholarship to Stanford Law School, but when she found herself pregnant at sixteen, she began to rethink the idea of going away to school. To make matters worse her baby,

Paige, was born with hydrocephalus, a disorder that causes an abnormal buildup of fluid in the brain. Because Paige's life expectancy wasn't long, Candace knew her time with her daughter would be limited. Stanford would have to wait.

Candace was an outspoken young girl with a firm sense of right and wrong, which is probably why she wanted to be a lawyer. She could be very confrontational and if she witnessed bullies or someone breaking the law, she had no problem speaking her mind.

Candace's brother Jimmy was nothing like her. He was a somber and quiet young man, and when their father died he struggled to cope with the loss. Jimmy fell into a world of drugs, alcohol, and suffered with very deep depression. He sank so low that he couldn't hold a conversation of more than a few sentences. Over time Jimmy withdrew from the family, unable to communicate with anyone at all. He packed a backpack and a tent and lived in the enormous wooded area of Colorado on his own.

In the summer of 2006, Candace and her mother Delores were driving toward their home on Copper Gulch Road when they passed two vehicles parked on the side of the rural road. Candace recognized both vehicles: One was a local Sheriff vehicle of an officer who was rumored to be corrupt. The other was a well-known meth cook (producer of methamphetamine drugs) in the area. As they passed the vehicles, Candace and her mother both witnessed the drug cook handing the Sheriff's deputy a thick envelope. In Candace's opinion, it was clear that a payoff or some sort of bribe was taking place. Candace was livid when she saw this, but with no proof there was nothing she could do.

A few days later in early August there was a knock at the door of the Hiltz home. Delores answered the door: It was the same Sheriff's deputy and he was looking for Jimmy. The deputy told her they believed Jimmy had been breaking in and burglarizing homes in the area.

The accusation upset Delores. She explained that Jimmy lived in the hills behind their home, had severe mental problems, and could never break into other people's homes because of his condition. Jimmy had been in and out of Colorado Mental Health Institute for severe social phobia and anxiety. She told the officer that Jimmy could barely speak to people and could never deal with that kind of confrontation. It was impossible that he could have been breaking into homes.

When the deputy called Delores a "damned liar" Candace overheard and ran to the door in a rage. She screamed at the deputy who told her that if she didn't calm down, he would arrest her. Candace reacted by holding out her wrists in front of her and yelled,

> "Go ahead! I will scream at the top of my lungs, 'what the hell are you doing taking envelopes from the drug cooks up here?'"

The deputy was furious, but speechless. He angrily turned and stormed back to his vehicle and drove away.

Later that week the family dog, Jackson, went missing. Jackson was a house dog, and it was rare that he got outside unattended. On the occasions that he did get out, he wouldn't venture far from the house. Candace and her mother called and searched for the dog all day, but Jackson was nowhere to be found. When several days had passed and Jackson hadn't returned, they assumed that a mountain lion, which were common in the area, had possibly attacked him.

Five days after Jackson had gone missing, Delores drove into town to run some errands and left Candace alone in the house to look after Paige. That afternoon around 3:20 p.m. Delores arrived home to find that someone had broken the back door open and she could hear Paige crying in one of the bedrooms. As she walked into the hallway, she knew something was dreadfully wrong. There was blood all over the hallway.

As she entered the first bedroom she saw that Paige was in her crib, crying, but at least safe. Delores then ran further down the hallway into Candace's room. There was blood pooling on the floor, but initially she didn't see any sign of Candace. It was then that she noticed that the bed was slightly angled and raised at one end.

Underneath the bed it looked as if someone had shoved a large green quilt under the bed, causing the inclination of the bed. But when she tugged at the quilt, she soon realized the disturbing truth. Candace had been shot point-blank in the face, head and chest, rolled into the quilt and callously stuffed beneath the bed. A shotgun shell was found in front of the fireplace in the living room.

Just days after accusing a Fremont County Sheriff's deputy of taking bribes, the Fremont County Sheriff's Office was now in charge of investigating Candace's murder. Two detectives were assigned to the case: Detective Harry Sharp and Lead Detective Robert Dodd.

Delores was questioned only briefly, and it seemed to her that Dodd really didn't have an interest in what she had to say. It was evident that he already had a suspect for the murder: Her son, Jimmy Hiltz.

Police quickly developed their theory. They believed that Jimmy had broken down the back door of the house intending to kill his sister. One of houses that they suspected Jimmy of breaking into previously was missing a shotgun. They believed he had shot Candace with that gun and then stuffed her beneath the bed and fled.

Delores knew their assumptions were absurd. Jimmy was just not the type to go on a rampage like that. He loved his sister and had no reason to kill her. In any case, Jimmy wouldn't have needed to break down the door. He had his own key and could come and go anytime he liked.

Despite her contention, police started a multi-agency search for Jimmy Hiltz for the murder of his sister Candace.

Search teams canvassed the endless acres around the home. After five days of searching, police found the family dog, Jackson, dead with the leash still attached to his collar; he had been missing for over a week. From the amount of decomposition, it was clear someone had killed Jackson not long after he had gone missing.

Detectives assumed that someone had removed the dog from the house so that the killer could more easily get into the house to kill Candace. This made the murder premeditated. To Delores, it assured her even further that this was not the work of Jimmy. Jimmy loved the dog and would have no reason to have killed him.

Three days after they found the dog, police found Jimmy Hiltz camping in the woods. He was unarmed and had no idea police had been looking for him. Detectives spent days interrogating Jimmy, but he refused to confess to the murder or the string of burglaries they had accused him of.

Detectives Dodd and Sharp had no physical evidence against Jimmy. Without DNA, ballistics, or blood evidence, they had no reason other than their own hunch to charge him.

Jimmy was charged with burglary, but was eventually deemed insane and unable to defend himself. He was admitted back to the Colorado Mental Health Institute for an indeterminate amount of time until he was mentally stable enough to stand trial.

The fact that he was mentally ill only furthered the detective's belief that he was the killer. Delores, however, knew that wasn't true and was worried that his mental illness and the pressure of the accusations would drive him to consider suicide.

Years passed by and no other suspects emerged. The case remained open, but no additional investigation was ever done on the case. Seven years after Candace's murder, Paige died from complications of her disease.

———

When a person rents a storage unit and fails to pay the rent, the contents of the unit go up for auction. Without knowing what's inside, anyone who's interested can bid on the contents, hoping that whatever is inside is worth more than they paid for it.

Ten years after the murder, Rick Ratzliff attended an auction for an abandoned storage unit in Cañon City, Colorado. With a bid of only $80, Rick won the auction and clipped the lock off of the unit.

As Rick rummaged through the contents of the storage unit he was puzzled to find an envelope marked "Evidence".

When he picked up the paper envelope a small axe dropped through the bottom of the deteriorating bag. Another bag marked "Evidence" contained a rope. Both the rope and axe were still covered in blood.

Inside the storage unit, Rick also found a box full of old police uniforms. When he held up one of the uniforms he noticed the name sewn into it read "Dodd." Rick knew the name and realized he had purchased Detective Robert Dodd's abandoned unit. He had remembered his name from hearing the news reports of Candace's murder ten years prior.

Astonished as to why the highest ranking detective in the Fremont County Sheriff's Office would have crime scene evidence in a personal storage locker, Rick handed the evidence over to the Colorado Bureau of Investigation.

The CBI verified that the items were indeed evidence from the Candace Hiltz murder investigation. Detective Dodd claimed he stored the items intending to take additional photos of them, but it slipped his mind.

When the story of the recovered evidence hit the local news, public pressure on the Sheriff's Office mounted and in January 2017 Robert Dodd was put on paid administrative leave.

The public also demanded more answers as to why there had never been charges brought against anyone for the murder. Because of the media pressure, police finally released the pathology report on Candace's murder.

The general assumption of the media and public had been what the police had told them: That Jimmy Hiltz had murdered his sister, but still could not stand trial due to his mental illness. But when the autopsy findings were released, public opinion quickly turned away from that assumption.

The autopsy showed that Candace had been killed with three separate weapons. She had been shot point-blank in the face with a shotgun. Then she was shot five times in the back of the head with a .22 caliber rifle. Lastly, she was shot in the chest, directly through the heart, with a medium caliber handgun.

Astonishingly, the Fremont County Sheriff's Office stuck by their theory that the murder was pulled off by Jimmy alone, despite any physical evidence pointing toward him.

Robert Dodd succumbed to the pressure of the media and public accusations and decided to move to Texas. When he was packing to move he had asked for a small dumpster to be parked in the driveway in front of his home so he could throw away the things he didn't want to move. After he had filled the dumpster he called Penrose Landfill to come pick it up and take it away.

Rob Orton was an employee for Penrose Landfill and was charged with picking up the dumpster from Dodd's property. Knowing Dodd's notoriety, Rob was curious of the contents of the dumpster. When he got it to the landfill and dumped it he noticed some strange items in amongst the garbage.

Not only did Dodd not go through the proper chain of evidence when he put the items in his personal storage locker, but he had also brought items home and later dumped them in his garbage.

Rob called a local reporter who had been covering the story and invited her to the landfill to go through the evidence before they called the Colorado Bureau of Investigation.

Together Rob and the reporter took photos of the items that Dodd had thrown away. They found a toolbox marked "Forensic Light Kit - FSCO Crime Scene Unit," assorted evidence DVDs, an FSCO laptop computer and more than twenty VHS video tapes labeled "Sexual Assault Evidence."

There were also envelopes full of sexual assault statements taken from victims. Many of the statements were from children who had drawn pictures of their attackers in crayon. Dodd had determined that this was evidence that could just be thrown in the trash.

It surely seemed that Robert Dodd had something to hide. In May 2017 he was charged with Official Misconduct.

At Robert Dodd's trial it was revealed that just days after the Candace Hiltz murder evidence was found in the storage locker, Dodd had logged into the official computer archive report of the murder and edited it six times. He had deliberately altered the case file with false information.

It was also revealed at trial that some evidence from the storage locker pointed to an additional person of interest in Candace's murder. The person of interest, however, was never revealed. Even if the person of interest had been revealed, the evidence had never been tested for DNA and because of degradation, was now useless.

Dodd's defense claimed that the Sheriff's Office had no specific policies or procedures for the handling of evidence. In July 2019, Robert Dodd was found guilty of two counts of Official Misconduct and abuse of a public record. He was sentenced to a $1,000 fine and 15 days of incarceration, but never spent a day in jail.

Because of this case and several others, eleven additional officers within the Fremont County Sheriff's Office were placed on administrative leave.

Twelve years after her death, no one has ever been charged with Candace's murder and Jimmy Hiltz is still a patient at Colorado Mental Health Institute; he also works there as a counselor for other patients.

CHAPTER 7
TAKING A CHANCE

Anyone living in the Phoenix area in the late eighties or early nineties is sure to remember Rick Chance. Rick's commercials ran continuously on every channel for many years. His business, Empire Glass, replaced car windshields, but he did it with flair and a marketing gimmick that worked amazingly.

The desert landscapes of Arizona meant lots of small rocks. Tiny rocks fly on the endless Phoenix freeway system, resulting in chips and cracks in car windshields. Rick Chance saw a massive opportunity. In 1982, he made deals with insurance companies and local restaurants to create Empire Glass.

Rick was the spokesman in his own commercials. He advertised that he would replace your windshield when it cracked at little or no cost to you and give you twelve free dinners at a nice restaurant for the trouble. Who's going to turn that down? Nobody. It was a massive success—so much so that after two decades, what started as a one-man operation, had expanded into six states was raking in $25 million a year.

Rick grew up in Maricopa, Arizona, a tiny farming town just south of Phoenix, and always had an entrepreneurial spirit. As a young boy his father wanted him to follow in his footsteps and encouraged him to work their farm with the tractor, but Rick told his father,

"Dad, I don't need to do this. I'm going to be a millionaire."

At an early age he lost an eye to childhood glaucoma and wore a glass eye, but that only seemed to empower him. Rick lettered in basketball, football, and track at Maricopa High School and edited the school newspaper.

Rick became enormously successful at business, but his love life was a train wreck. In January 1979, Rick married Norrie Ann Rose. Within three months she had filed for divorce. He talked her out of the divorce initially, but it was destined to end, and in 1981 they divorced just before he started Empire Glass.

A year later he married Christine Gay Pyland. His marriage to Christine lasted longer and spawned two children.

Rick Chance lived his life being pulled in two directions. He loved the millions that his business made for him and thrived on extravagance. He owned a multi-million dollar home in the affluent neighborhood of Paradise Valley, drove a top-of-the-line Mercedes, and despite the Arizona heat, occasionally wore a sable coat. He wore expensive jewelry and frequently went to strip clubs.

On the flip-side, Rick was deeply religious and could quote long bible verses verbatim. He donated vast sums of money to charities and regularly gave money to evangelical churches, as well as funding international ministries. He believed his success was directly related to his relationship with the Lord.

After ten years of what seemed to be a picture-perfect marriage, his relationship with Christine was in trouble. Rick met a nine-teen-year-old prostitute at The Phoenician resort who drugged him and stole $71,000 worth of jewelry and his Mercedes. Christine filed for divorce, shared custody of the children and moved to Denver. In court documents she accused him of "wasteful and frivolous spending" and ignoring his family.

> "He is frequently out of town and spends sixty hours per week in work and work-related activities…Rick was in an extremely embarrassing legal situation involving a prostitute which, unfortunately became front-page news."

Christine was awarded control of the Denver operation of Empire Glass, half of their Paradise Valley home, a $20,000 fur coat, her 1991 Infiniti convertible, and Rick was to pay for their children's private religious school tuition.

Though viewing himself as deeply spiritual, being drugged and robbed, and going through a rough divorce, Rick continued to flash his wealth and showed his vulnerability. The second marriage, however, was nothing compared to the third.

In 1995 Rick met a stunning green-eyed blonde named Jill Scott. Jill was a beauty queen that had won the title of Mrs. America in 1990. Rick married Jill on Valentine's Day in a fairy tale wedding that was broadcast live from Las Vegas on Good Morning America.

Jill, however, had some secrets of her own. Shortly after winning the Mrs. America title she was sued by the pageant because she was actually separated from her first husband at the time, making her ineligible for the title of Mrs. America.

She also hid from Rick the fact that she had had several plastic surgery operations and had signed a contract to star in a pornographic movie called, "Mrs. XXX-America." He filed for an annulment after only four months of marriage.

The judge threw the annulment out, but he filed for another in 1998 where he described his wife as a "gold digger," whose goal was to, "divest him of his assets and leave."

But Jill had no shortage of accusations against Rick. She claimed that she thought she was marrying a good Christian man, but found herself with a "religious kook" who would chant incantations, and order her to read scripture for hours while bent over, face-down, holding her ankles in adoration of God.

"When I say chanting, I mean he would repeat a prayer over and over again, or a phrase of his own, over and over again."

She claimed that Rick once received a complaint letter from a customer and screamed, "This is from Satan," then ripped it up, threw it on the fire and started chanting.

She also spoke of unusual sexual demands that Rick would ask for, claiming she once walked in on him in their bedroom with another man, both naked with towels wrapped around their waists.

She recalled, "He seemed to be battling his inner demons. His desires were strong and went against his spiritual life."

By the time divorce number three was over in 1998, Jill was awarded $250,000, jewelry, and $8,333 per month for four years.

Though Empire Glass was still making him millions, Rick was getting bored with the glass business. His real passion had become jewelry, and he was determined to make his next fortune as a jewelry dealer.

A tight group of dealers operated the "jewelry circuit" in the Phoenix area and Rick had some trouble jumping into an already established industry. He sold his expensive jewelry to local dealers and low-end jewelry he would sell through newspaper ads.

Rick would buy wholesale from dealers and middlemen, then turn them around, selling them as his own designs. But his favorite jewelry he couldn't design himself—Rolex watches and raw diamonds.

Despite three failed marriages and being robbed, Rick was still overly trusting of people and would often carry a brief-case full of jewelry with him to show to clients in public places. A friend, David Hans Schmidt, recalled their evening at the cigar bar of The Ritz-Carlton in Phoenix:

> "We were drinking Chambord liqueur at $9.50 a pop until it was coming out of our ears. I got up to go to the bathroom and, I swear, I came back and there's Rick's briefcase open on the table. There's a half million dollars' worth of jewels sitting here and he's at the bar talking to some bimbo."

Rick was very trusting of everyone, and whenever friends warned him that showing off valuables in public like that can make him a target he would scoff, "… eh, it's all insured." But one friend recalled telling him, "Yes, but insurance isn't going to cover your ass."

Rick and Schmidt would frequent the strip clubs of Phoenix together and Rick would pay the $600 fee for the two of them to go to the VIP Champagne room with the girl of their choice. One of their favorite strip clubs was Christie's Cabaret on 32nd Street. Rick preferred Asian girls and Christie's was where Rick met Brandi Hungerford.

————

Brandi Hungerford was born in South Korea in 1977 and adopted by an American family when she was only a few weeks old. She grew up in a typical Midwest setting in Grand Rapids, Michigan with eight brothers and sisters.

In 1995 Brandi moved to Tempe, Arizona with the intention of attending Arizona State University, but before she got a chance to enroll she saw an ad in the newspaper that read, "Looking for Models." ASU was put on the back-burner when she realized she could make $1,200 a week as an escort.

Brandi's father had developed cancer and much of the money she made stripping and escorting went to help with his care. Her father's illness and what she was doing for a living began to change her emotionally, according to her friends. The girl that was once happy-go-lucky, now kept things bottled-up; she became moody and indifferent.

Brandi worked the full-range of adult establishments in the Phoenix area. Christie's Cabaret was a more "high-end" strip club, while Bourbon Street was a little darker and seedier. She also worked at a "bikini club" called Southwest Attractions, a two-story building in an industrial area near the airport with no windows. Inside, after being checked for weapons, customers choose a girl and are escorted to a private room for thirty minutes of "companionship." The company also offered an outcall service, where a girl would meet a client in a hotel room of their choosing, usually accompanied by a male bodyguard waiting in the car outside.

———

Rob Lemke was a tall high-school dropout from Spanaway, Washington, just south of Tacoma. He was known for his hot temper and his passion for guns and Asian girls. His rap-sheet included felony assault, illegal weapons possession, and parole violation.

Lemke moved to Arizona in 1999 with his girlfriend to avoid sentencing for a weapons charge in Washington State. His girlfriend helped him buy an assault rifle since he couldn't buy one legally with his felony conviction. Once established in Arizona he became a male stripper and escort. He was 220 pounds of muscle and became quite popular at male strip clubs like the Hideaway.

As a male stripper, Lemke was known to cross the line legally. He wanted a fast-lane to wealth and was willing to get there any way he could. Legal or not. Lemke started his own escort agency, which is how he met Brandi Hungerford, and the two started dating.

Brandi had been out with Rick Chance a few times; he was very open with her about his wealth and showed her the briefcase of jewelry he carried around. When she told Rob Lemke about the briefcase he instantly saw dollar signs.

Lemke put together a plan for he and Brandi to steal Rick's briefcase full of jewelry, but their first attempt was a failure. Rick had met Brandi for Mexican food before they went back to his house. The plan was for Brandi to call Lemke and tell him to come to his house and rob him, but Rick and Brandi had spent the evening smoking pot in his $3 million Paradise Valley home and when she called Lemke, she was too high and mumbled into the phone that she couldn't remember the street he lived on.

Throughout the summer of 2002 Brandi left Rick several messages, most of which he didn't return. Brandi and Lemke thought Rick may have become suspicious of her. The unanswered calls would later become a trail of evidence for police to use against her.

In early August 2002, Rick and Brandi went out a few more times. After dinner on the evening of August 8, Brandi suggested they get a bottle and have some drinks at the Best Western hotel in Tempe. Brandi later recalled,

"Rick probably thought he's gonna get sex."

After checking in at the front desk, Rick and Brandi entered room 317 and Rick lit a cigar while Brandi stepped into the bathroom. He had no idea she was in the bathroom calling Lemke to give him the room number. When Brandi emerged from the bathroom, she told Rick she would step out into the hall to get some ice from the ice machine. In the hallway, Lemke was waiting for her. He put on a black ski mask and gloves, took her keycard, and entered the room with a gun in his hand.

At 1:15 p.m. the following afternoon it was well past check-out time. A maid at the Best Western ignored the "Do Not Disturb" sign and entered room 317. Rick was face down on the floor, lying in a pool of blood.

When police arrived, they found a single shell casing, an orange pill, white powder and a burned stick of incense. Rick Chance had a single bullet wound in his throat. In his pockets were his identification, credit cards, some cash, two wrapped condoms, and the keys to his 2000 Mercedes. The briefcase with over $1 million in jewelry was missing.

The forensic evidence came easily. Brandi's keycard was left in the room with her fingerprints on it. Her fingerprints were also on the hair dryer. Surveillance video showed Brandi and Rick in the parking lot, at the front desk, and in the hallway of the third-floor room. Rob Lemke was in clear view of the security cameras just outside their door too. Police shared photos with the media, and the calls poured in.

Of the hundreds of calls that came in to police, one was particularly useful: A call from Brandi's mother who worked as an officer at the Maricopa County Estrella Jail. She had recognized her daughter on the local news channel and called Tempe police.

When police searched Brandi's cell phone records, it showed multiple calls to Rob Lemke. The Tempe police then searched Lemke's Tempe apartment and found jewelry tags that displayed Rick's brand.

It wasn't difficult to ascertain that Rob was originally from Washington State and already had a warrant out for his arrest. All law enforcement agencies between Arizona and Canada were alerted to be on the lookout for Brandi and Lemke.

Police were correct in assuming they'd run back to Washington State. Brandi and Lemke had fled to Tacoma, where Lemke knew someone who he thought would buy the jewelry from him.

Five days after the murder, Brandi was arrested in Tacoma without incident. Lemke was arrested just two days later. They were found with jewelry, a fur hat filled with more than $20,000 in cash, and several guns.

Brandi was charged with first-degree murder and was cooperative during her interrogation. She provided the murder weapon to police and fingered Rob as the trigger-man. The gun that killed Rick had been given to a friend of Lemke and hidden inside a pizza box.

Brandi told police that she had no idea Lemke planned to kill Rick. She said that after leaving the room she stood in the hallway for less than a minute before she heard a loud pop,

> "I peek around the corner and at some time I heard pop, and it scared me. It sounded like a gunshot."

A witness in a nearby room, however, contradicted Brandi's explanation. The witness told police they heard her say,

> "Don't hurt him. He's not going to say anything."

The witness claimed that she then looked through the hotel door peephole and saw a man standing guard.

For her cooperation in implicating Lemke, prosecutors offered Brandi a lesser charge of second-degree murder, along with armed robbery, and conspiracy charges. She accepted the offer. Brandi Hungerford was sentenced to fourteen years in prison, serving part of her term at the same prison that her mother used to work. She was released in August 2016.

Rob Lemke fought extradition without success. When he was returned to Tempe to face charges, he eventually pleaded guilty and was handed a life sentence. He will be eligible for parole in 2032.

CHAPTER 8
THE TIGER PARENTS

"Tiger parenting" is a term used to describe a style of strict, demanding parenting, popular within the Chinese community. Every parent wants their child to achieve greatness of some sort, whether it be sports, the arts, or academia, but a tiger parent is a completely different animal. Tiger parents are obsessive with their child's success and push their influence on their children to the extreme.

A typical tiger parent would expect their child to attend an Ivy League school like Harvard, Princeton, or Yale. They also might regulate who their child dates, so they marry into a "good" family. Ultimately, their goal is to make sure their child gets a lucrative job such as Wall Street lawyer, investment banker or highly paid surgeon.

Huei Hann Pan and Bich Ha Pan were stereotypical tiger parents. Hann had immigrated to Toronto, Canada as a refugee and his wife Bich (pronounced "Bick") followed shortly after. The two married after their arrival in Canada and got jobs working for an auto parts manufacturer. By the late eighties, they had two children, Jennifer and Felix.

The Pans led an extremely thrifty life, saving as much as they possibly could. By 2004 they had $200,000 in the bank and owned a nice-sized home in a suburban neighborhood. Their sole extravagancies were their cars, a Mercedes and a Lexus. Their main objective was to save enough to send their kids to the best schools and make sure they were eligible for any possible scholarships. They wanted to make absolutely sure that Jennifer and Felix lived a more plentiful life than they did.

Their first born, Jennifer Pan, showed potential at an early age. By the age of four she was already taking piano lessons, proving to be exceptional. In her elementary school years, she started figure skating. Some evenings Bich and Hann would keep her up practicing until 10:00 p.m. —and then homework until midnight.

At graduation from middle school Jennifer was expected to be valedictorian of her class, but was turned down. She was devastated and her parents even more so. The pressure on Jennifer was immense—more than a girl in her early teens could handle. She told her friends that she would just put on her "happy mask," but deep down she was suffering and began cutting her forearms with tiny cuts.

Jennifer attended high school at Mary Ward Catholic Secondary School in Toronto. The school was known for its unique self-directed learning program with uncommonly high academic standards. Jennifer fitted in well and got along with almost everyone. Her parents monitored her after-school activities closely in which she became an avid swimmer and practiced Wushu, a Chinese form of Kung Fu. In band class, Jennifer excelled at playing the flute.

Though she was an accomplished ice skater, her skills began to slip. A second-place in a skating completion just wasn't enough for her demanding parents and her confidence began to slip. At one point she was an Olympic hopeful in figure skating, but those hopes were quashed when she tore a ligament in her knee.

In earlier years Jennifer was a straight-A student, but by the end of ninth grade her grades in everything but music had slipped considerably. Knowing that a C or even a B wasn't going to sit well with her parents, Jennifer got creative. Armed with her old report cards, glue-stick, scissors, and a quick trip to Kinko's she was able to create the straight-A report cards that her parents expected. But she knew she would have to improve her grades before the final two years of high school if she wanted to get into college.

Jennifer's activities out of school were closely monitored by her parents. Even into her twenties, she had never been allowed to go out with friends without close supervision. She had never been drunk or gone to a nightclub. She felt as though she was missing out on her childhood and the controlling nature of her parents infuriated her.

In her junior year of high school Jennifer traveled with the school band to Europe playing the flute. When the band played an auditorium that allowed smoking Jennifer had an asthma attack. A fellow student and trumpet player, Daniel Wong, took her outside and calmed her down.

Daniel was a chubby, funny, and happy-go-lucky kid. He was also a part-time pot dealer. When he took the time to take care of Jennifer, it impressed her, and it wasn't long before they were dating. But of course, she would have to hide the relationship from her parents.

By the time senior year rolled around, Jennifer's grades still hadn't improved and she had continued forging her report cards. She had already been accepted to attend Ryerson University the following year, but when she failed her calculus class Ryerson dropped her. Not only was she not going to be going to University, she wasn't even going to graduate from high school with that failing grade.

Nervous that her parents would find out, Jennifer continued forging documents. As far as they knew, she was going to Ryerson. She told them she would take two years of science and then would transfer to the University of Toronto's Pharmacology program, just as her father had planned. Her father, Hann, was ecstatic and bought her a new laptop for school.

Jennifer forged receipts for tuition and a $3,000 scholarship, bought used textbooks, and left every morning for school. But instead of going to school, she took the bus downtown and hung out at cafes and public libraries all day. She studied scientific subjects and filled her notebooks with notes as if she was attending class. She also spent time with Daniel, who was attending York University. She taught piano lessons when she could and worked part-time days at the pizza place where Daniel worked as the kitchen manager.

When Jennifer arrived home in the evenings, she made up elaborate stories about her lessons, teachers, and other students. She told very few friends of the huge lie she was telling her parents, knowing that if friends knew it may eventually get around to her parents.

Eventually Jennifer convinced her parents to let her move in with her friend Topaz three nights a week. Topaz lived closer to campus and she wouldn't have to make the long commute every day. But this was just another lie on top of all the others. She actually moved in with Daniel and his parents. His parents constantly asked to meet with her parents, but she made excuse after excuse.

After two years of lying to her parents about Ryerson University, it was time for her to transfer to the University of Toronto. She found someone online to print her a fake transcript.

Graduation from Ryerson was going to be tricky. Jennifer came up with an elaborate excuse that her graduating class was too large and students would only be allowed one guest. Rather than choose between her mother and father, she gave her guest invitation to a friend so that both of her friend's parents could attend.

Jennifer's parents still didn't even know that she had a boyfriend; if they had known, they would have forbidden it. Though she lived with Daniel three nights a week, she wanted to stay more. She told her parents that she was going to volunteer at Toronto's Hospital for Sick Children in their blood testing lab so she would need to stay in the city on the weekends as well.

This was the first time that her parents suspected her of lying. Her father knew that if she was working at the hospital, she would need a uniform and a keycard, but she didn't have them. Hann convinced his wife Bich to follow her, but Jennifer knew she was being followed. Jennifer went to the hospital and sat in a waiting room all day until she was convinced that her mother was gone.

Her parents still knew that she was up to something and the next morning they confronted Topaz who broke the news to them that Jennifer had never lived there and was instead living with Daniel.

When they confronted her, Jennifer confessed. She told her parents that she wasn't volunteering at the hospital, she wasn't attending University of Toronto, and she was staying with Daniel. But she still didn't tell them that she had never attended Ryerson University and hadn't even finished high school.

Jennifer's father was beyond livid. His first instinct was to kick her out of the house, but her mother, who was much more lenient than her father, intervened. Her parents forbade Jennifer from leaving the house for two weeks. During her time at home, Jennifer's mother spent as much time as she could with Jennifer. Though her father had taken her phone away from her and insisted on no contact with Daniel or any friends, her mother occasionally let her have access to her phone.

In February 2009 Jennifer wrote on Facebook,

> "Living in my house is like living under house arrest. No one person knows everything about me, and no two people put together knows everything about me... I like being a mystery."

Eventually she got access to her phone and though she was forbidden from having any contact with Daniel ever again, she would sneak phone calls and texts, and she would occasionally sneak out of the house. Every chance she got between teaching piano lessons, she would sneak to Daniel's house.

Her parents eventually allowed her to retake her calculus class to get the one last credit she needed to get her high school diploma. Then she would need to apply for any school that would take her. Her father was convinced that it wasn't too late and she could still become a pharmacy lab technician or a nurse.

Meanwhile, Daniel was getting sick of all the sneaking around. She was twenty-four years old, but her parents had full control over her love life. Eventually Daniel broke up with her and started seeing another girl, Christine.

Jennifer grew insanely jealous and concocted an elaborate story to regain his attention. She told Daniel that a man had come to her door claiming to be a police officer and showing his badge. When she opened the door a group of men pushed their way into her home and gang-raped her. She then told him that the following day she had received a bullet in the mail. Jennifer told Daniel it was all a warning from his new girlfriend; she claimed Christine was trying to keep them apart.

By the spring of 2010 Jennifer had had enough. Her father was tearing her life apart, and she wanted it to end. She wanted her parents dead. In high school she had heard stories of a boy named Andrew Montemayor. The rumor was that he had robbed people at knifepoint and had once considered killing his own father. She contacted Montemayor but he wouldn't have anything to do with her plan, but told her that his roommate Ricardo Duncan might be interested. According to Jennifer she paid him $1,500 that she had earned from teaching piano but then never heard from him again.

Jennifer and Daniel were texting again, and she shared her thoughts with him. She explained that her parents were worth about $1 million and if they were out of the picture she was set to inherit $500,000. If her parents were dead, she and Daniel could live their life with no sneaking around and they could finally be happy.

During his weed-dealing days Daniel had met a guy named Lenford Crawford who went by the nickname "Homeboy". Daniel thought that if anyone knew how to hook something like that up, it would be Homeboy. Sure enough, he did. Daniel set up a meeting between Jennifer and Crawford and they agreed on a price. Crawford told her the going rate was $20,000, but for a friend of Daniel he would only charge $10,000. Jennifer agreed and said that once she got her inheritance it wouldn't be a problem.

Crawford gave Jennifer an iPhone and a SIM card. This phone and SIM would be used strictly for when they spoke and would then be destroyed after the deed was done.

Though Daniel knew of the plan and knew Jennifer's deepest, darkest secrets, he was still in love with Christine. He told Jennifer he wanted out of the plan. She texted him:

> Jennifer: "So you feel for her what I feel for you, then call it off with Homeboy."
>
> Daniel: "I thought you wanted this for you?"
>
> Jennifer: "I do, but I have nowhere to go."
>
> Daniel: "Call it off with Homeboy? You said you wanted this with or without me."
>
> Jennifer: "I want it for me."

The next day Daniel confirmed it was all still going to happen.

> Daniel: "I did everything and lined it all up for you."

Despite Daniel professing his love for Christine, his flirtatious texts still continued in the days after.

In early November 2010, Crawford texted Jennifer,

> "I need time of completion. Think about it."

> She replied, "Today is a no go. Dinner plans out. We won't be home in time."

Eventually Crawford and Jennifer agreed on a date; Monday, November 8.

At 9:30 p.m. on Monday night, Bich Pan had just returned home from a night of line dancing with her friends. Her husband Hann had retired early and was already in bed. Jennifer's younger brother Felix was away at college, and Jennifer was in her bedroom watching television. Bich kicked off her shoes and filled a footbath with warm water to soak her feet and watch some TV in the living room before going to bed.

At 9:35 p.m. Jennifer came downstairs, asked her mother about her night, kissed her goodnight, and discreetly unlocked the front door. She then went to her bedroom, and spoke on her iPhone for three and a half minutes.

At 10:02 Jennifer turned an upstairs bedroom light on, then one minute later turned it off. That was the signal that the door was unlocked. Jennifer then sent a text:

> "VIP Access."

Moments later three men came through the unlocked front door: Lenford "Homeboy" Crawford, David Mylvanganam, and Eric "Sniper" Carty. All had guns drawn.

One man ran up the stairs to the room where Hann was sleeping and put a gun in his face. He demanded that Hann go downstairs where another man was watching over Bich.

Bich and Hann spoke to each other in Cantonese, wondering what they wanted when one of the men yelled,

"Shut up! You talk too much! Where's the fucking money?"

Hann assured him he only had $60 in his wallet and Bich pleaded with her assailants, "Please don't hurt my daughter."

The third man, Carty, went up the stairs and met with Jennifer outside of her bedroom. Jennifer handed him $2,500 in cash and showed him another $1,100 that her mother kept in her nightstand. He then tied her arms behind her back with a shoelace and led her downstairs with her parents.

The men took Jennifer back upstairs and tied her to the stairway railings while they took her parents downstairs to the basement.

Moments later, five shots rang out. Hann was shot twice. Once in the face and once in the shoulder. Bich was shot two times in the back and once in the head. Though Bich died instantly, Hann was bleeding profusely but still alive. After eighteen minutes in the house, the three men left through the front door and left Jennifer alive upstairs.

Jennifer's Samsung flip-phone was tucked into the waistband of her pants. Despite being tied with her hands behind her back, she pulled the phone out, flipped it open, and dialed 911.

"Help me, please! I need help! I don't know where my parents are!... Please hurry!"

'What's your name?"

"My name is Jennifer."

"Someone just broke in?"

"Someone broke in and I heard shots like pop. I don't know what's happening. I'm tied upstairs."

"Did it sound like gunshots?"

"I don't know what gunshots sound like. I just heard a pop."

(screaming in the background)

"I'm ok! My Dad just went outside screaming."

"Do you think your mom is downstairs too?"

"I don't hear her anymore. Please hurry, I don't know what's happening."

The screaming that was heard thirty-four seconds into the 911 call was Hann Pan. Covered in blood, Hann crawled out of the basement and back to the main floor of the house. He then ran outside, screaming as loudly as he could. Nearby neighbors heard his screams and called 911 as well.

When police and emergency crews arrived to the home, they found Jennifer upstairs tied to the bannister just as she had said, her flip-phone laid on the floor next to her. Hann Pan was rushed to the hospital where he was put into a medically induced coma.

At 3:00 a.m. Jennifer was brought in for her first interrogation. She told police that three black males had burst into the house, had taken whatever cash they could find, and had shot her parents. Police asked her to explain how she managed to pull her flip-phone out of her waistband while tied to a bannister. She demonstrated that she reached around her waist, flipped the phone open with her thumb, and turned the volume all the way up.

She showed that making the call was possible, but still left a lot of unanswered questions. If it was a robbery, why did they leave so many valuable items in the house? Why did they not bring duffel bags or backpacks to carry what they had stolen? Why did they not take the Lexus or the Mercedes when the keys were there in plain view? How did they get in the front door so easily? If they had planned on killing two people, why leave a third as a witness?

The biggest question police had was: Why did Hann come up the stairs and run outside for help, when he knew his daughter was still in the house? Why did he not try to help her? Their questions would be answered a few days later.

Detectives set up twenty-four-hour surveillance on Jennifer and even followed her to her mother's funeral. During the funeral detectives noticed she had a lack of tears or emotion as they lay her mother in the ground.

When Hann awoke from his induced coma, his neck bone was shattered, bones in his face were broken near his eye, there were bullet fragments lodged in his face, and a bullet had clipped his carotid artery. Though he was barely alive, Hann remembered everything and had a story to tell that differed greatly from the story Jennifer told.

Hann told police that Jennifer's story was all lies, like everything else about her life. He said that when the men rushed in he was taken downstairs at gunpoint into the living room with his wife. When he looked for his daughter Jennifer, he saw her speaking in a friendly manner with a white man and walking around the house with him without any restraint.

Police had already interviewed Jennifer twice, but on
November 22 brought her in for a third interview. Two
hours into the interview Detective Bill Goetz began what is
referred to as the Reid Technique.

The Reid Technique is a controversial interrogation procedure that was developed in the fifties to evoke a confession.
It has been banned in most European countries because it
involves deceptive techniques such as lying to the suspect
about the evidence against them and invading their personal
space. The procedure has been accused of leading to many
false confessions, but it's still in use in most of the United
States and Canada.

Using this technique, Goetz falsely told Jennifer that police
used satellites and infrared technology to view activity
within buildings and they had software that could tell if a
person was lying.

Jennifer succumbed to the interrogation and admitted that
she hired the men, but not to kill her parents. She told police
she hired them to kill her. She claimed that she had tried to
commit suicide many times in the past but had failed every
time. She said she had hired a hit on herself, "I didn't want to
be here anymore."

She told police that her parents wouldn't allow her to see
Daniel Wong anymore and she wanted to end her life. She
said the men were already outside the house when she
decided to call it off, but they demanded the money anyway
and burst into the house. She claimed that she couldn't pay
them, so they shot her family instead.

The cops didn't buy her story; they arrested her and brought
Daniel Wong in for questioning. Daniel confirmed that she
was lying once again, as she did with everything in her life.

Despite Jennifer destroying the SIM card, police were able to recover text messages from her iPhone and Daniel's phone to confirm her arrangement with the hitmen. Jennifer, Daniel, and the three hitmen were charged with first-degree murder, attempted murder, and conspiracy to commit murder.

Jennifer's trial lasted almost ten months, and she took the stand in her own defense for seven days, but it was no use. When she was handed the guilty verdict she initially showed no emotion. Once the cameras left the room, she burst into tears and shook uncontrollably.

Jennifer Pan was sentenced to life in prison with no chance of parole for twenty-five years. Daniel, Mylvaganam, and Crawford all got the same sentence. Jennifer was also given a non-communication order. She was no longer allowed to have any contact with the other defendants or anyone in her family.

When Carty's lawyer became ill, his trial was declared a mistrial and was postponed. In December 2015, Carty pleaded guilty to conspiracy to commit murder and was sentenced to eighteen years in prison with parole eligibility after nine years.

Hann Pan still suffers with his injuries and is unable to work. He released a statement after the trial which read,

> "When I lost my wife, I lost my daughter at the same time. I don't feel like I have a family anymore. Some say I should feel lucky to be alive, but I feel like I am dead too. I hope my daughter Jennifer thinks about what has happened to her family and can become a good honest person someday."

CHAPTER 9
MOM, I'M A MONSTER

Just northwest of Denver and southeast of Boulder lies the suburb of Westminster, Colorado. The city of about 100,000 is a nice, safe place to raise a family. At least that's what the residents thought before May 2012.

On the Memorial Day holiday, a twenty-two-year-old woman was jogging around beautiful Ketner Lake, a fifty-acre open space with a one-mile trail that encircles the lake. As she ran along the secluded trail in the early afternoon, a man ran up to her from behind, grabbed her arms, and forced a cloth over her mouth. She could smell the distinct odor of chemicals on the cloth.

The young woman was lucky. Though she was terrified, she was strong enough to fight the man and got away to call police. She described the attacker as a white male, approximately five feet eight inches tall, with brown hair, an average build, wearing a blue baseball cap, black t-shirt, jeans, and sunglasses.

Westminster police developed a sketch of the attacker and obtained some DNA from the scene, but months went by and they weren't able to find any suspects.

Police had no idea the attacker was seventeen-year-old Austin Sigg. When Austin was just twelve years old his stepmother sent him to a faith-based therapist after finding porn on his computer. He wrote a note to his therapist,

"I have an addiction to porn, and I would like to stop."

This wasn't just any kind of porn, though. Austin was addicted to child porn.

Austin went through therapy and his therapist encouraged his father to add parental controls to his computer, but as with any teenager nowadays, he easily circumvented it. From there, his addiction only escalated.

Austin later recalled,

"… it took a hold of me and it just started growing. After I got done seeing my Christian therapist, psychiatrist, whatever you want to call it, I thought I had a grip for a little while and then it probably lasted not even a month and then I went back to it."

To his friends and fellow students, he seemed like a relatively normal kid. Friends said he was a bit of a goth kid, but well-liked, smart and "a total sweetheart." He had a collection of swords and knives, but came across as a regular kid into music and video games. His classmates, however, had no idea about the crazy thoughts that were swirling in his head.

Austin left high school early to attend Warren Tech, a local technical school, and get his GED high school equivalency.

He then enrolled at Arapahoe Community College. He wanted to put high school behind him and pursue his obsession: Mortuary science and crime scene investigation.

In addition to his porn addiction, Austin had an obsession with dead bodies and decomposition. He took dead rats home from school so he could study them in various stages of decomposition.

Austin's father was a wealthy business owner, but had a long criminal record. Robert Sigg had a federal conviction for bank fraud and various other charges including assault, burglary, domestic violence, distributing drugs, DUI, and resisting arrest.

By the time Austin reached seventeen, his child porn obsession had progressed to include violence and death. On his iPhone, Austin kept photos and videos of children, bondage, rape, and human dismemberment.

————

On October 5, 2012, five months after the Ketner Lake jogger was attacked, ten-year-old Jessica Ridgeway started her walk to school just like any other day.

Jessica was excited to become a teenager. Only three more years. She loved to play waitress and cheerleader; she loved math, and her favorite color was purple. She was known for her purple glasses and the tiny gap in her front teeth.

Jessica's mother worked the night shift from 10:00 p.m. until 7:00 a.m. so she was able to see Jessica off to school in the morning before she slept during the day.

Normally Jessica walked to school with a young boy down the street and called the boy's father at 8:25 a.m. to let them know she was on her way. Jessica kissed her mother good-bye, put on her black puffy coat, and at 8:30 a.m. headed out the door. Though the boy only lived a few houses away, Jessica never arrived there. The boy's father assumed Jessica's mother had decided to drive her to school.

When Witt Elementary School realized Jessica had not shown up for school they called her mother, Sarah, but because of her work schedule, she was still asleep and the call went to voicemail.

When Sarah Ridgeway woke at 4:00 p.m. and heard the voicemail, she immediately went looking for Jessica along the route to school. She checked her friend's homes, the nearby parks, but there was no sign of Jessica.

> Sarah Ridgeway told the media, "... and then you get a pit in your stomach you don't want any parent to experience in their entire life. When you know your child has been taken."

Jessica's terrified mother reported her missing at 4:30 p.m. and the search started immediately. Police questioned school faculty and went door-to-door along her route to school, hoping for any leads.

Volunteers and firefighters joined in the search and an amber alert was issued at 9:15 p.m. By morning there were over a thousand people searching for Jessica, resulting in one of the largest searches in Colorado history.

Police sent divers into Ketner lake while sniffer dogs and helicopters searched the area, but there was no trace of Jessica. Despite their efforts, the first forty-eight hours came and went with no clues.

On Sunday, October 7, six miles away, a man found a backpack in his yard. Not having heard the news of the missing girl, he posted on a local social media page about it and mentioned that it contained a key chain with the name Jessica Ridgeway. Others in the group informed him that was the name of the missing girl, and he turned the backpack over to police.

Inside the backpack investigators found Jessica's purple glasses and the clothes she was wearing when she left for school that morning. Her clothes were soaked in urine. DNA analysis of the backpack revealed the DNA of someone other than Jessica. Most likely it was the DNA of her abductor. When the DNA was put through databases, it revealed that it was also a match to the DNA from the person who attacked the jogger on Ketner Lake.

Five days after Jessica had gone missing, maintenance workers were working in Pattridge Park Open Space when they noticed something that seemed strange and out of place. In a patch of tall whisky grass was a large black garbage bag. When workers opened the bag, they found a tiny human torso.

Pattridge Park was nine miles southwest of Jessica's home in the town of Arvada. Arvada police and Westminster police worked together with the FBI under floodlights throughout the night processing the scene.

The torso was missing the arms, legs, and head and had been wiped clean, but not clean enough. Police were able to retrieve DNA from the torso. It matched the backpack and the Ketner Lake jogger.

The next morning, investigators announced the devastating news. The torso was indeed the remains of ten-year-old Jessica Ridgeway.

A sense of anguish and terror gripped the community of Westminster and the surrounding cities. Parents took time off work to make sure their children made it to school safely. The city that once left doors unlocked and kids played free had instantly lost its sense of security.

Jessica Ridgeway's funeral was held on October 16, and her favorite color purple was predominant. Over 2,000 people attended. Her mother wore a purple ribbon in her hair, mourners released purple balloons, and Colorado Governor John Hickenlooper wore a purple shirt as he spoke and expressed the sadness of the entire state of Colorado.

In the days after Jessica's death over 700 local residents gave voluntary DNA samples. One of those samples was seventeen-year-old Austin Sigg. He had been studying crime scene investigation and was confident he had left no trace, so he voluntarily allowed investigators to swab his cheek. Incredibly, Austin's DNA sample was mishandled. His DNA was mistakenly returned to police in a batch of samples that were not a match.

Three days after the funeral, on October 19, Westminster police asked the public for help. They had found a small cross near the torso in Pattridge Park, which was possibly part of a necklace. Police were asking for anyone that may have seen the cross before to come forward, and they were in luck.

A woman called detectives and reported that a friend of hers, Mindy Sigg, had a son who wore a cross similar to the one shown on the news and lived less than a mile from Jessica's home.

When police interviewed Austin Sigg, he was calm and answered all questions asked of him. He told police he was sleeping on the morning that Jessica disappeared.

Though he was calm during the questioning, after the interview he was on edge and told friends at Arapahoe Community College that he felt "sick and wobbly." Austin was certain that the FBI had matched his DNA to the samples taken from the torso and the backpack. On the night of October 22, Austin was panicking, and so slept with his mother.

The next day Austin told his mother, "I am a monster and need to be punished." He explained what he had done, and his mother called Westminster police. The following are excerpts from Mindy Sigg's 911 call:

————

Mindy Sigg: "Hi, um, I need you to come to my house... um, my son wants to turn himself in for the Jessica Ridgeway murder."

911: "And what's going on there. Ma'am, are you there?"

Mindy: "Did you not hear me? He just confessed to killing her."

911: "I know. I want you to tell me what's going on. Can you tell me exactly what he said?"

Mindy: "That he did it and gave me details and her remains are in my house."

The 911 dispatcher then asked to speak to Austin.

Austin Sigg: "I don't exactly get why you're asking me these questions. I murdered Jessica Ridgeway."

911: "Okay."

Austin: "There is… I have proof that I did it… there is no other question. You just have to send a squad car, something down here."

Austin Sigg also admitted to attacking a jogger at Ketner Lake. He was then asked if he had weapons.

Austin: "I have knives in my room, um, and we own a few guns, but… I'm giving myself up completely, there will be no resistance whatsoever."

The dispatcher talks again to Mindy.

911: "Is Austin still there with you?"

Mindy: "Yeah, I'm hugging him (crying)."

911: "Okay, you guys are hugging? Okay, you definitely did the right thing. You tell me when the officers get there, they're coming to your front door, okay?

(The complete sixteen-minute 911 call is available in the online appendix at the end of this book.)

———

Investigators questioned Austin Sigg for hours while he explained in horrific detail how he abducted and murdered Jessica Ridgeway.

Austin had been hiding in the back seat of his Jeep on the morning of October 5 as Jessica was walking to school. Though he claimed Jessica was chosen at random, he had parked near her house and knew that she would have to walk past her house and knew that she would have to walk past his vehicle as she walked down the street. As she passed his Jeep he leapt out of the back seat and grabbed her. Jessica screamed, but nobody heard her screams.

Using zip ties, he bound her wrists and ankles and threw her in the back seat, then drove down random side-streets. By the time they arrived at his house, the frightened ten-year-old had wet herself with fear.

Austin claimed that he sat with Jessica for two hours in his bedroom watching a movie and cartoons and she asked him over and over if he knew her mom. He then cut her hair and gave her clothes to change in to. He put her urine soaked clothes into her backpack. Initially he claimed he didn't sexually assault her, but later admitted that he did several times. She suffered considerable bruising from the force of the rape.

After he had repeatedly raped her, Sigg told her to face the wall. When she turned around he put zip ties around her neck in an attempt to strangle her. He told investigators that he "didn't have enough leverage" with the zip ties and they cut into his hands. He then tried strangling her with his bare hands, but after three minutes he realized his hands just weren't strong enough. Eventually he filled the bathtub with scalding hot water and forced her head underwater, drowning her.

Sigg went on to tell investigators that he shoved the small cross into her vagina and dismembered her body, using a small knife and a saw. He cut her arms, legs, and head off. Police didn't release full details of the dismemberment, but

Sigg told detectives that the whole process fulfilled a sexual fantasy for him.

He cut her hands and feet into small pieces and flushed them down the toilet. He then removed her internal organs, put them into containers and labeled them. He kept her skull and organs in a small crawl space in his home.

Sigg told police that afterwards he sat looking at her body,

> "All I could think of was, 'Oh god, what have I done?'…
> There is no better word to describe what I have done than evil."

At only seventeen years old at the time of the murder Sigg could not be charged as an adult and wasn't eligible for the death penalty or life in prison because the Supreme Court determined those penalties are cruel and unusual punishment for minors. Instead, he was charged in Juvenile court, but prosecutors wanted to make certain he would never again see the outside of a prison.

The counts against him piled up. He was charged with nineteen counts, including first-degree murder after deliberation, three counts of felony murder, sexual assault on a child, second degree kidnapping and robbery, plus attempted murder, attempted kidnapping, and attempted sexual assault for the Ketner Lake jogger attack. Sigg pleaded guilty to all counts against him.

His defense argued that he was not mature and didn't understand the acts he was committing, but the judge disagreed. On November 20, 2013 Austin Sigg was sentenced to forty years in prison for first-degree murder plus an additional eighty-six years for the remaining eighteen counts against him, ensuring he will never be released from prison.

On October 5, 2013, one year after her death, the city of Westminster Colorado changed the name of Jessica's favorite park to the Jessica Ridgeway Memorial Park. Throughout the park the sidewalks are etched with Jessica's favorite knock-knock jokes and the children's playground toys are painted her favorite color, purple.

CHAPTER 10
A GRISLY NEW ORLEANS TALE

Z ach Bowen grew up like any other normal American boy. He was sociable and had an average number of friends. Nothing about him made him extraordinary. For the most part he led a normal American life. It wasn't until he turned eighteen that his life started to change.

Just after his eighteenth birthday, before he was legally allowed to drink, Zach met twenty-eight-year-old Lana Shupack in a New Orleans strip club. Though she was ten years older than him they dated and eventually married and had two kids together.

In order to support his new family, Zach decided his best option was to join the US Army. He enlisted in the 709th Military Police Battalion and was sent on a tour of duty in Kosovo and a second one in Iraq, spending time in Abu Ghraib. Back home, Lana sent him strip club photos of her and her coworkers.

Though he later almost never spoke of it, Zack experienced atrocities that left him with post-traumatic stress disorder. During the early days of his first tour a member of Zack's unit, a young female friend, Rachel Bosveld, was killed during a mortar attack in Baghdad. The death drained him mentally and the once happy-go-lucky man fell into a more somber tone.

Later in his military career, Zack became friends with a young Iraqi boy. When insurgents blew up the shop that the boy's family owned Zack fell into an even deeper depression.

Zack had been promoted to sergeant and when it was time to leave the military his commanding officer gave a recommendation for an honorable discharge. But much to Zack's disappointment he was given a general discharge, making him ineligible for GI Bill education benefits. In addition to his depression, Zack felt cheated for his service in the military.

By the time Zack returned to New Orleans, his marriage had failed. Though they didn't divorce, he and Lana separated and Zack took a job as a bartender in the French Quarter. It was during that time that he met Addie Hall who also worked as a bartender in the trendy area of New Orleans.

Addie was artistic and free spirited. She wrote poetry and occasionally taught dance classes. She was described by her friends as "a mean drunk," and "… a wonderful person, except when she wasn't." According to her friends, Addie had been molested as a child and was a victim of several abusive relationships; she also suffered from bipolar disorder.

Zack and Addie moved in together and started their tumultuous relationship. Both were heavy drinkers and drug users, and Addie was known for her abusive temper. Together the couple had a passion for both drinking and fighting. When they were drunk or high on cocaine Addie could easily turn a minor argument into a raging inferno.

Zack and Addie became an iconic couple during Hurricane Katrina. While the rest of the city had evacuated and camped out in the Louisiana Superdome, the two decided not to vacate. They stayed in their apartment that they rented above the Voodoo Spiritual Temple on Rampart Street and drank their way through what seemed to be the end of the world. The national news media interviewed them and their story was featured in the New York Times.

They seemed to thrive on the lifestyle that the hurricane brought. To them it was like a camping trip. No electricity and plenty of booze. They didn't have to work, they could drink all day, and they didn't have any bills to pay. Addie would occasionally flash her breasts at passersby just to make sure the police regularly patrolled their street.

In early October 2006, a year after Hurricane Katrina, the two twenty-eight-year-olds got into one of their epic fights. Addie was convinced that Zack had been cheating on her. On October 4, she approached the landlord of their apartment and asked to have Zack taken off of the lease. Knowing Addie's explosive temper, the landlord refused, tried to calm her down, and suggested that she try to patch things up with Zack.

———

Two weeks later on October 17 at 8:30 p.m. a man looking out the window of his hotel room at the Omni Royal Orleans Hotel in the French Quarter noticed a man's body on the roof of the adjacent parking garage.

Police arrived to find the body of Zack Bowen face down on the roof. His body was mangled and lifeless, clearly having died from the impact, but police were unsure if he had been pushed or he had jumped. Small cigarette burns were found all over his body. When police searched his pockets looking for identification, they found a note that said:

> "This is not accidental. I had to take my own life to pay for the one I took.

> If you send a patrol to 826 N. Rampart, you will find the dismembered corpse of my girlfriend Addie in the oven, on the stove, and in the fridge along with full documentation on the both of us and a full signed confession from myself.

> The keys in my right front pocket are for the gates. Call Leo Watermeier to let you in.

> Zack Bowen."

When police arrived at the Rampart street apartment, the first thing they noticed was the temperature. The air conditioner was running full-blast. It had been turned down to sixty degrees, presumably to slow the rate of decomposition.

The walls of the apartment had been spray painted with red paint,

> "Please call my wife. I love her."

> "I'm a total failure."

> "Look in the oven."

> "Please help me stop the pain."

On the stove was a pot with Addie's charred head in it. In another pot were human hands and feet. A roasting pan inside the oven contained arms and legs. All were burnt beyond recognition. Potatoes and carrots were cut up on a cutting board next to the stove. Investigators noticed what seemed to be Cajun seasoning on the limbs, but from the burnt condition of the body parts, it's believed his intention was not to eat them. It's assumed Zack cooked the body parts in an attempt to remove the tissue from the bones for easier disposal.

In a large plastic garbage bag inside the refrigerator was the torso of Addie Hall.

Addie kept a journal and Zack had filled in the last eight pages. It was a confession in horrifying detail of how he had killed his girlfriend.

> "Today is Monday 16 October 2 a.m. I killed her at 1 a.m. Thursday 5 October. I very calmly strangled her. It was very quick."

> "Halfway through the task, I stopped and thought about what I was doing. The decision to halt the first idea and move to Plan B (the crime scene you are now in) came after a while. I scared myself not only by the action of calmly strangling the woman I've loved for one and a half years, but by my entire lack of remorse. I've known forever how horrible a person I am (ask anyone)."

The note mentioned that he had had sex with her body several times after strangling her and would drink in the apartment with her body until he passed out. He went to work as usual. When he got home from work, he moved her body to the bathtub and dismembered her with a handsaw and a kitchen knife. When police arrived, the bathroom had been thoroughly cleaned.

In his suicide note, Zack also explained the cigarette burns on his own body. He had burned himself one time for each year of his life as a punishment for his failures.

Zack Bowen had demons of his past war experiences and there's no place like New Orleans for a demon story. In the years afterwards, the house at 826 N. Rampart became a tourist attraction, infuriating the couple's friends and family.

Eight years after the murder/suicide, a documentary was made called "Zack and Addie." The film featured a woman named Margaret Sanchez. Margaret was a friend of both Zack and Addie and spoke of her relationship with the couple and of the nightmares she still had in the years after. She hypothesized that Addie may have killed herself rather than Zack killing her.

On June 6, 2012, in a disturbing twist to the story, Margaret Sanchez and her boyfriend Terry Speaks walked into a New Orleans strip club called "Stilettos" and asked about getting a threesome with one of their dancers for a private party. Unable to find a willing girl, they went to another bar called "Temptations." There someone pointed them in the direction of a young girl with purple hair named Jaren Lockhart. They told the couple she was desperate to make some money.

She was indeed desperate and quickly said yes to their proposition. Jaren was seen on security cameras grabbing her belongings from the dressing room and primping herself in the mirror, then she exited the building with the couple. She was seen with the couple a few additional times on Bourbon Street security cameras, then she was never seen alive again.

Jaren Lockhart's dismembered body parts washed ashore days later on various beaches in Mississippi. There were mutilated areas where tattoos had been, which was an attempt to hide her identity.

When Sanchez and Speaks were arrested Speaks' computer had recently been wiped clean. His car reeked of cleaning products. In e-mails between the couple they spoke of a rare celestial phenomenon called the Venus Transition, when Venus passes directly in front of the sun, that happened at the exact time of the murder.

Cadaver dogs reacted to scents in the couple's back yard, shrubbery, burn pile, and a trash can. Inside the burn pile, investigators found remnants of women's underwear and pieces of a cell phone. Several parts of Jaren Lockhart's body were never recovered.

During the trial the forensic pathologist explained her death and dismemberment in graphic detail. Members of the jury were seen openly weeping.

Terry Speaks was convicted of second-degree murder and sentenced to two life sentences. One day later Margaret Sanchez pleaded guilty to manslaughter, obstruction of justice, and conspiracy to obstruct justice. She was sentenced to forty years in prison.

CHAPTER 11
THE ALLIGATOR THEORY

At the southwest corner of Georgia where it meets the border with Florida, the Chattanooga and Flint rivers join to form Lake Seminole. The lake was artificially formed by the Jim Woodruff Lock and Dam in the fifties. From there, the water flows 500 miles south through the Apalachicola River toward the Gulf of Mexico.

The shallow water was full of stumps from trees that were there before the lake was formed. The stumps created problems for boaters that used the lake for fishing and duck hunting. But that didn't discourage thirty-one-year-old Mike Williams. Every chance he got, he would make the fifty mile drive from Tallahassee, Florida to go to his favorite duck-hunting spot.

Mike got his first taste of duck hunting when he was fifteen. In high school Mike was a jock. He was a star football player, student body president, and was active in the Key Club. North Florida Christian School was also where he met the love of his life, Denise Merrell, who was a cheerleader at the same school.

Denise and Mike dated, and after high school Mike went on to Florida State University in Tallahassee where he majored in political science and urban planning. He worked his way through college as a property appraiser where his boss, Clay Ketcham, said he was the "Hardest-working man I ever saw."

Mike and Denise married in 1994 and in 1999 had a baby daughter they named Anslee. By 2000 Mike had built a real estate business and was making over $200,000 a year.

December 16, 2000 was a special day for Mike and Denise. It was their sixth wedding anniversary. They had plans to celebrate that evening, but Mike wanted to start the day with a quick trip to the lake for some duck hunting. It was mid-December and very cold and stormy, but he was determined to get some hunting in. Mike woke up early, grabbed his gear, loaded up his Ford Bronco and towed his boat out to Lake Seminole before dawn.

Leaving that early in the morning, Mike should have been home long before noon, but when he hadn't returned home that afternoon Denise was frantic. Mike wasn't answering his cell phone, so she called her father who then called Mike's best friend, Brian Winchester. Together, the two men drove out to Lake Seminole late that afternoon to look for Mike.

When they arrived at the boat launch where he usually parked, his Bronco was nowhere to be found. They searched the area, and just before nightfall they found his Bronco and boat trailer parked seventy-five yards away at a muddy boat launch that he normally would never use. It would have been very unlike Mike to park there when his normal boat launch was available. As darkness fell, the wind picked up, and the temperature dropped to nineteen degrees. The wind and pouring rain made a further search impossible, so they waited until morning.

The next day Denise's father, Brian Winchester, and the Fish and Game Department continued their search for Mike. That morning they found Mike's boat about 300 yards from the boat launch. Strangely, it was 300 yards in the opposite direction that the strong winds had blown that night. Inside the boat was a shotgun still in its case, although it wasn't the shotgun that Mike normally used for duck hunting. They also found hunting equipment and duck decoys, but there was no sign of Mike.

Searchers assumed that Mike's boat may have hit a stump in the lake and that he had been thrown overboard with his hip-wader boots on. Divers were sent to search the murky lake; helicopters scoured the lake from the skies, hundreds of man hours were put in by several law enforcement agencies. Days turned into weeks and weeks turned into months, but Mike had simply vanished.

Because the lake was filled with stumps and his hip-waders were missing, law enforcement assumed that Mike had fallen overboard and drowned. His boots had most likely filled with water and pulled him under. The lake was also known for being alligator infested and it was believed that after he drowned he had been eaten by alligators. The case was treated only as a missing persons case.

Six months later a hunting cap was found floating on the surface of the water. Police thought it might have belonged to Mike Williams and sent divers into the area. In the same area they found his hunting vest, his still-working flashlight, his hunting license, and his pair of hip waders.

In the state of Florida, a missing person can only be declared deceased if they've been missing for five years. But only eight days after Mike's belongings were found in the lake, Denise Williams successfully petitioned the state to have his death certificate issued. With the valid death certificate she was now able to collect Mike's two life insurance policies totaling over $1,500,000.

As the years went by, Mike's mother, Cheryl Ann Williams, wasn't buying the accidental death theory. She saw several gaping holes in the "official" story and started her own investigation.

Cheryl wanted a criminal investigation opened into his disappearance, but Mike's widow, Denise, threatened to cut off access to her granddaughter, Anslee, if she did. Ultimately, Cheryl lost access with her granddaughter and pursued the death of her son.

The first thing that stood out to Cheryl was that none of the items found six months after Mike's disappearance seemed like they had been submerged for six months. The hat and jacket were pristine and free of mud or algae. The hip wader boots had no teeth marks—nothing to indicate an alligator attack. Even his hunting license was still legible after spending a supposed six months in the murky lake.

She also contacted alligator experts that supplied her with an important fact. Alligators don't feed in temperatures below forty degrees, they go into a state called brumation. Similar to hibernation, alligators become lethargic and their metabolism slows down significantly. They dig themselves into a bank of the lake and go dormant until the weather gets warmer. The temperature when Mike disappeared in December was well below freezing. There was no possibility that he could have been eaten by alligators.

Additionally, alligators don't eat people whole. When alligators do attack humans, they bite, chew, and tear the bodies. There are always pieces left to be found. In the history of Lake Seminole there had been a total of eighty deaths there. Mike's death would have been the only one in which a body had not been found.

There were other inconsistencies Cheryl found. Mike's boat was full of gasoline when it was found. If he had fallen out of the boat while it was running, the boat's motor was designed to circle endlessly until it ran out of gas.

Mike's friends also verified that he would never have worn his hip waders while driving the boat. He would only put them on once he reached a hunting spot.

The most significant sign for Mike's mother was the fact that his widow, Denise, was issued a death certificate after just six months and awarded the life insurance claim. There were two policies, one of which was for $1 million written just six months before he vanished. The insurance agent that sold him the policy was his best friend, Brian Winchester.

Five years after Mike's disappearance, Brian Winchester and Denise Williams were married.

———

This solidified Cheryl Williams' suspicions. Mike Williams was not in that lake. She knew it. She spent years trying to get investigators to take a second look at the case.

Every Sunday Cheryl could be found in Bradforville holding a giant "Missing" sign on the side of the road in the hope that someone might see his face and remember something. She took up donations and paid for huge billboard signs, flyers, posters, and websites. Nothing seemed to help.

Cheryl never gave up. She sent over 240 letters to the then-Governor of Florida, Rick Scott. Every single letter went unanswered.

She regularly placed full-page ads in the Tallahassee Democrat newspaper:

An open letter to Governor Rick Scott:

> Dear Governor Scott,
>
> Fifteen years ago, today, December 16, 2000, my son, Mike Williams, supposedly drowned in Lake Seminole, Sneads, Florida, while on a solo duck/hunting trip.
>
> After a two-week search of the lake, Mike's body was never found. I was told by Florida Fish and Wildlife Conservation Commission Officers, that my son fell out of his boat, drowned, and was eaten by alligators.
>
> Governor Scott, there is only one problem. Alligators do not eat in cold water. They hibernate! It would have been physiologically impossible for an alligator to eat anything, much less a 5'10" 180 lb. man.
>
> Mike was declared dead six months after he disappeared when (planted) evidence surfaced in the lake. His wife collected millions of dollars in life insurance, and then married his best friend.
>
> It took me three and a half years to get a criminal investigation into Mike's disappearance, because of this investigation I lost access to his daughter.

FDLE has been the lead investigating agency since February 2004. I still do not know what happened to my son. His case is now considered an active cold case, nothing is being done to find Mike or his murderers.

In May 2012, in a face-to-face meeting, in front of witnesses, I was told by an FDLE investigator, "Ms. Williams, you no longer have an investigation because you don't do things the right way!" In other words, Governor Scott, I talk too much.

Governor Scott, I have written a letter to you every day since you took office. You do not see my letters because they are sent over to FDLE, the very agency I am complaining about.

Governor Scott, would you please appoint a Special Prosecutor from another part of the state to investigate my son, Mike's disappearance? As a parent yourself can you image the undying agony of not knowing where your daughters are for the past fifteen years, while simultaneously being lied to, ignored, and being called crazy by law enforcement officials, when the facts clearly prove otherwise?

Please help me find my son,

Cheryl Ann Williams

Cheryl's efforts fell on deaf ears, but she never gave up hope.

By 2016 the marriage between Denise and Brian Winchester was falling apart. Things had begun to sour in 2012 due to Brian's sex addiction, and Denise filed for divorce in 2015.

On August 5, 2016 just before the divorce was to be finalized Winchester told a friend that he thought the police were "after him" and that once she divorced he was convinced that she would,

"say something about this guy who died 10 or 12 or 15 years
ago."

Brian Winchester hid in the back of his wife's car and waited
for her to arrive. When she got into the driver's seat she felt a
gun barrel jammed in her side as he climbed over the seat.

Winchester grabbed her phone and told her to drive. He told
her that because she had blocked his text and refused to take
his calls, he had no choice. He held her against her will for
over an hour until she finally pulled into a drugstore parking
lot and parked next to the front door. He threatened suicide
if she divorced him, telling her he had nothing to live for.
Eventually she talked him down and agreed to not tell the
police he had kidnapped her.

After he released her Brian apologized for what he had done
and she drove straight to the police station. Brian Winchester
was arrested for kidnapping, domestic assault, and armed
burglary. Two of the charges were felonies. Denise asked for
a restraining order and claimed she was so distraught that
she hadn't been able to eat or sleep for weeks. Winchester
was held without bond.

Mike's mother was elated with the news of Brian and
Denise's breakup and after sixteen years it gave her new
hope that she might be able to find out what had happened to
her son,

> "Brian's not going to let Denise run around alone with all
> that money. I'm praying he doesn't commit suicide; I'm
> praying he'll tell us what actually happened."

She added that she was alone among her family in holding
out hope that her son was still alive.

Brian Winchester sat in jail for over a year awaiting trial. During the trial the prosecuting attorney told the media that he hoped that the case would help solve the disappearance of Mike Williams, but there was no mention of Mike at all during the court proceedings.

Finally, in December 2017, Winchester was sentenced to twenty years in prison for the kidnapping plus another fifteen years of probation. The day following Brian's sentencing, the Florida Department of Law Enforcement called a press conference. They had found the body of Mike Williams.

After seventeen years, Mike Williams' remains were found buried at the end of a dead-end road just five miles from where he grew up, forty miles from Lake Seminole.

The body had actually been discovered two months earlier in October. As part of a plea deal, they had waited until after Brian Winchester's sentencing to announce it.

Florida Department of Law Enforcement brought thirty workers to the area to work sixteen-hour days for five days without even telling the workers what they were looking for. The search was to be kept confidential and workers were told it was a training exercise. The work involved digging nine-foot-deep holes with a backhoe and building dams and pumping water to keep the nearby mucky Carr Lake from destroying their work. Investigators searched through massive stacks of mud and found 98% of Mike Williams' bones. DNA from the bones matched that of his mother.

On May 8, 2018 Denise Williams was arrested as she was on her way to her daughter's nineteenth birthday. She was charged with first-degree murder, conspiracy to commit first-degree murder and accessory after the fact. Remaining details were kept confidential until court.

Prosecutors argued that Denise Williams conspired with Brian Winchester to kill her husband as early as nine months before his death. At court prosecutors played an audio recording of the police interview with Brian Winchester after his kidnapping arrest. Brian confessed to killing Mike Williams in cold blood, but claimed the whole thing was Denise's idea.

Brian Winchester took the stand to testify against Denise where he told the court he had been having a relationship with Denise ever since high school. They both married other people, but continued their affairs off and on and frequently double-dated with their spouses. He explained that in 1997 their affair "snowballed" and they began a steady affair for the last three years of Mike's life.

Winchester explained that because of Denise's religion, her family would never forgive her for a divorce. Instead, she plotted to kill her husband. Denise suggested several methods of getting rid of him, such as faking a boating accident in the Gulf of Mexico for both her husband and Brian's wife, Kathy. But Brian didn't want his children to grow up without their mother. Other ideas involved a robbery at Mike's work, but they eventually agreed to make it look like a hunting accident.

On the day he disappeared, Brian invited Mike to Lake Seminole for a morning of duck hunting. Once they were out on the water Brian waited until Mike put on his hip-wader boots and pushed him out of the boat, assuming he would sink to the bottom. But Mike didn't sink. He held on to a tree stump. Brian finished the job by circling the stump in the boat and shooting Mike in the face with a shotgun.

With a shotgun blast to the face, the story of a boating accident wouldn't work. Winchester then pulled Mike's body out
of the lake, left the boat and belongings, and drove forty
miles away to bury Mike's body near Carr Lake.

Though there was no physical evidence linking Denise
Williams to the murder, that didn't stop the jury from
coming back with a guilty verdict on all charges.

The following February Denise was sentenced to life in
prison. Cheryl Williams addressed the media only to say that
justice had finally been served. Denise was allowed to sign
over the remainder of the insurance money to their daughter
Anslee in order to avoid prosecution for insurance fraud. As
part of the agreement, no part of the insurance money was to
be used for Denise's legal defense.

CHAPTER 12
THE KIČEVO MONSTER

Kičevo is a mountain plateau city of a little over 20,000 inhabitants. Throughout the years the area has changed hands many times, once belonging to the Byzantines, then conquered by the Ottomans, Serbia, Yugoslavia, and is now called Macedonia. Not much happens in Kičevo. It's a halfway point between the capital and fancy resorts on Lake Ohrid. Other than a pit-stop, there's not much reason to stop in the slow-paced town.

Though the area has seen its share of warfare throughout the centuries, it generally wasn't a place that was known for violent crime. Daily life in Kičevo was mundane and boring. Nothing much happened that was newsworthy. That was until three women between the ages of fifty-six and sixty-five were beaten, raped and strangled between 2005 and 2008.

The slayings were exciting news for Vlado Taneski. He was a mild-mannered journalist in his early fifties, frustrated with the lack of reportable news in the area. News of the brutal murders kept local residents riveted to the newspapers and Taneski's articles that covered them. He seemed to have an uncanny inside knowledge of the murders and an extreme eye for detail that kept residents buying papers.

Vlado Taneski was born in 1952 and raised in Kičevo to parents who were strict conservative disciplinarians. When his eldest brother left home, his parents disowned him and never spoke to him again. They did the same to his older sister. Vlado's father was a World War II veteran who worked as a security officer while his mother was a custodian at the local hospital. Both were extremely strict parents who often took a belt to their children whenever they misbehaved.

Vlado attended a technical high school, and after graduating took a job at a local factory. He was active in the local communist youth programs which allowed him to travel to central Croatia to attend political school where he studied journalism. In 1973 Vlado met his future wife at a poetry reading. He was twenty-one; she was nineteen, and both shared a love of literature. After four years of dating, the couple married and soon had two boys.

By the time he and his family returned to Kičevo in 1980, Vlado was more educated than most people in the city and factory work was beneath him. His wife had finished her law degree. He initially worked for Radio Kičevo, then advanced his career to become a journalist. He was a staff reporter for Nova Makedonija (New Macedonia), the largest daily newspaper in Macedonia, based in the capital city of Skopje.

Though his father was a loner, and he had a tumultuous relationship with his mother, Vlado moved his parents in with him and his family.

Vlado's wife later recalled,

> "His mother took her younger son's abandonment very hard.
> Then her daughter, Trajanka, went to work in Skopje. Vlado
> was the only child in the household left to take care of his
> parents. So when I married him, we both decided to stay and
> live with them."

Over time, Taneski became a very talented writer. Besides
his journalistic writings he also wrote poetry, short stories
and several novels. As technology progressed, he remained
nostalgic, longing for the old days of communism as opposed
to capitalism, and preferring a typewriter and paper over
computers.

Living in a small town outside of the capital and his
penchant for nostalgia both took a toll on his career and
Vlado was passed up for many articles. He was assigned to
cover stories taking place in his own small town. With such a
quiet town, this didn't leave much.

By 2003 his full-time staff position at the newspaper had
been eliminated and Taneski only worked as a freelancer,
selling a story whenever he could.

Though his parents lived in his home, Taneski's father spent
much of his time alone at the family summer cottage several
miles away, and in August of that year he hanged himself in
the cabin. Just four months later his mother accidentally
overdosed on sleeping pills.

Taneski's life had reached a low point, but journalistic work
was suddenly about to pick up in Kičevo.

In November 2004 a sixty-one-year-old retired custodian,
Mitra Simjanoska had gone missing. She lived in the same

neighborhood where Taneski had spent his entire life and he covered the story for the newspaper.

Theories swirled throughout the town about Mitra's disappearance. She was known to have many lovers. Had she made a man jealous? Did she run off with someone? In January 2005, the townspeople received some answers. As a man was looking through an abandoned construction site he came across the body of a woman in a large nylon bag. She had been dumped naked into a shallow hole in the ground.

Though Mitra had been gone for two months, her body showed only a few weeks of decomposition. She had obviously been kept alive somewhere. She had been raped, strangled, and her hands and feet were bound with a telephone cord.

Police were quick to find suspects. Just a month earlier in the nearby village of Malkoetz an elderly man had been robbed, raped, and murdered. The killers had tortured him by placing objects in his anus and took heated fireplace tongs to his penis. Two men in their twenties were charged with the murders.

Because the killing of the old man was similar to Mitra's death in that it involved extreme torture, the two men were charged with her murder as well. They pleaded guilty to killing the old man, but insisted they had nothing to do with the killing of Mitra Simjanoska.

In Vlado Taneski's article titled "Surgical Gloves for a Monstrous Murder" he wrote,

> "In handcuffs and with searching eyes, 28-year-old Ante
> Risteski and his friend Igor Mirčeski, accused of a horrible
> double homicide in Kičevo and Malkoetz, walked into the

courtroom. They stared vacantly at the ceiling and from
time to time whispered, as if to themselves: it's all over and
now we'll pay for our crimes."

The two young men were tried, convicted and sentenced to
life behind bars, but there were still unanswered questions.
Mitra's body was found with traces of semen, but the DNA
from the semen didn't match either of the men sitting in jail
for the crime.

Later that year, to make ends meet, Taneski's wife took a job
with the Ministry of Education in Skopje, seventy miles
away. She moved to Skopje and took their youngest son with
her while the eldest son went abroad to study. Taneski had
spent his life with a house full of family and suddenly found
himself completely alone. He took the time to start using a
computer for work and often spoke of selling the two Kičevo
homes, but that never happened.

In November 2007 another woman from Kičevo, Ljubica
Licoska, went missing. Like Mitra, Ljubica was also a custodian, an older woman, and coincidentally lived in the same
neighborhood as Taneski.

Ljubica's body was found three months later near a gas
station. She had been subjected to the same types of torture.
She was found wrapped in a plastic bag, bound with a telephone cord, and had been raped and strangled. Pathologists
determined that the body had only been dead for a few days,
but she had been missing for three months. Again, this meant
that she had been kept alive somewhere and endured three
months of rape and torture.

When the people of Kičevo realized the similarities between
Ljubica and Mitra, rumors started to swirl that the two men
who were locked up may not have been the killers.

People also pieced together similarities to an older case predating the others. Another elderly woman had gone missing in May 2003. Like Mitra and Ljubica, Gorica Pavelska was a seventy-three-year-old retired cleaner who also lived in the same neighborhood. When she went missing most people thought she had possibly gone to work in Skopje, but now there were rumors that all three cases were linked.

On February 6, 2008, Taneski's story was the top story in the Morning Herald,

> "Rumors abound. While the police are working on the case, the majority of people in Kičevo think that this murder is related to the double homicide in Malkoetz and Kičevo, when two older citizens were killed for a very small sum of money."

Taneski also speculated that Ljubica had possibly been hit by a car and rather than the driver taking her to the hospital he had decided to kidnap and torture her.

> He reported, "The Kičevo police have not announced a suspect yet, but, according to our sources, the investigation is on its way to solving the case."

Just three months later another body was found. Zivana Temelkoska was a sixty-five-year-old custodian at a local school. Again, she was from the same neighborhood as Taneski and the other victims with the same profession. Zivana's body was found near a soccer field on top of a trash heap. Her body was placed inside a plastic bag wearing only her nightgown. She had been savagely raped, bound with a phone cord and strangled.

Zivana had five broken ribs and thirteen cuts on her skull. She had been raped with a glass bottle and several other items including a vial of aftershave, cotton balls and gauze. Like Mitra, pathologists were able to retrieve semen from her body.

Taneski had interviewed police, detectives, neighbors and the victims' family members. His front-page article on May 19 read,

> "The people of Kičevo live in fear after another butchered body has been found in the town. The corpse strongly resembles one discovered 20 kilometers outside Kičevo last year and there is a possibility that these monstrous murders are the work of a serial killer."

> "Both women were tortured and murdered in the same fashion, which ruled out the possibility that there could have been two killers. The Ochrid serial killer murdered three people [in 2007] but his victims were all street-based money exchangers and his motive was to rob them."

> "The motive of the Kičevo monster remains unclear. Both women were friends and living in the same part of town. Police have a few suspects who they are interrogating."

> "The latest body was found in a rubbish dump. It had been tied up with a piece of phone cable with which the woman had clearly been previously strangled."

> "Officials from the Ministry of Interior say that they have several suspects, all of them from Kičevo. They were interrogated and released. There is confirmation that traces from the murderer have been found on both victims, and those are now being analyzed."

Realizing they had a serial killer on their hands, police developed a psychological profile of the killer. The murders were all planned well, and the killer showed an extreme amount of control. Their profile showed that the killer was likely a strong, middle-aged male with above-average intellect. They also believed he was sexually frustrated, most likely since childhood. From the killing they knew that his sexual frustrations had grown into sadomasochism. They also believed that the killer acted alone.

Next to Zivana's body, police found an old jersey with blood traces on it. The blood type was B positive - not hers.

Police interviewed over 150 men and eventually narrowed the list of men down; their next step was to test them for DNA that could match the semen samples. One of the suspects was Vlado Taneski himself.

Vlado had known all the victims. They all knew his mother and worked as cleaners, just as his mother had. But the thing that caught police's attention were his articles published in the newspaper. Taneski seemed to have information about the killings that had not been released to the public. Specifically, he reported that the telephone cord that was used to bind Zivana was also used to strangle her. Based on his knowledge of this information, Taneski was arrested on June 20, 2008.

After his arrest, independent forensic labs confirmed that his DNA matched the semen that was found on two of the victims. They also confirmed that they found seven hairs near Ljubica's body that belonged to Taneski. The old jersey found near Zivana's body belonged to him and the green nightgown she was wearing belonged to Taneski's mother, suggesting that he dressed the victims as his mother before raping and killing them. When police searched his house and summer cottage, they found some of the victims' clothing.

During more than twenty hours of interrogation, Taneski was mostly silent. The questions he did answer were mostly vague claims that he couldn't recall.

Due to lack of space Taneski was transferred to the jail in the nearby town of Tetovo and placed in a cell with three other inmates. The cell had two bunk beds and a separate bathroom. Inside the bathroom was a large white bucket.

At 2:00 a.m. on June 23, one of the cellmates alerted guards when he found Taneski on the bathroom floor. His head was in the bucket of water, and his hands were to the sides. Guards tried to revive him, but Taneski was pronounced dead.

Inside his pockets were three items: a round trip train ticket to Skopje that he had purchased before he was arrested, several pills of the anti-depressant Paxil, and a signed note that read,

> "I have a note under the pillow on my bed."

The note under his pillow was a suicide note proclaiming his innocence,

> "I have not killed the women. I am proud of my family."

The sudden death of Taneski left more questions than answers. The ability to hold one's head in a bucket long enough to drown is nearly impossible, but his body showed no defensive wounds that would indicate he was forced into the bucket. There were also no signs of a struggle.

Conspiracy theories of the case spread throughout Macedonia. Was he a victim of waterboarding? Were the police protecting the real killer? His military record shows his blood type was O positive, which was different to the blood found on the old jersey. Ultimately, there was no motive for the police or other cellmates to want him dead. The police wanted to see him tried in court. The only person to benefit from Taneski's death was Taneski himself by avoiding a lifetime in jail.

CHAPTER 13
BONUS CHAPTER: THE HOMESCHOOLERS

This chapter is a **free bonus chapter** from True Crime Case Histories: Volume 5

———

It's not clear what life was like for Hana Alemu in Ethiopia, but it's hard to imagine it could have been worse than it became when the eleven-year-old was adopted by the Williams family in Sedro-Woolley, Washington.

———

Larry and Carri already had seven children of their own and wanted more, but her last pregnancy had left Carri Williams unable to bear more children. It had become a trend for homeschooling evangelical Christians in the mid-2000s to adopt needy children into their already large families. The families felt that it was a duty of their faith to rescue children that needed a good home and then homeschool them according to a conservative Christian curriculum. Other families from their Bible study group had adopted as many as eight children into their lives; Carri and Larry wanted the same.

Larry Williams worked from noon until midnight as a millwright for Boeing, while Carri stayed home to homeschool their kids. Carri had attended a women's retreat run by a ministry called Above Rubies. During the retreat, they spoke of the trend among evangelicals to adopt children from Liberia, a west African country experiencing political instability caused by multiple civil wars.

In 2008, the Williamses contacted Adoption Advocates International (AAI), a secular adoption agency based in Port Angeles, Washington. AAI was run by a woman named Merrily Ripley who had twenty children; three biological and seventeen adopted. Merrily informed Carri that there were two orphaned children in Ethiopia that needed a loving home. One child was deaf and Carri had studied American Sign Language before getting married, so it seemed like a perfect match.

To prepare for the adoption, the Williamses took a quick home-study course provided by AAI and filled out the necessary paperwork. AAI apparently missed the fact that Carri had left one section of the paperwork blank: the part about their beliefs on child discipline.

———

In the months leading up to the adoption, Carri and Larry saw a one-minute video clip of the children crying and begging for a good home. It was heart wrenching. Seven-year-old Immanuel was deaf and eleven-year-old Hana was slightly underweight at only 77 pounds.

Immanuel and Hana had been living in the Kidane Mehret orphanage in the Ethiopian capital city of Addis Abada. Both had been abandoned at an early age. Though they were not related, they were excited that they would soon become brother and sister living in the United States. Learning that their new parents lived in the idyllic countryside of the Pacific Northwest, Hana naively read *Little House on the Prairie* in preparation for her new, exciting life.

In the months after Hana and Immanuel's arrival in 2008, the Williams' post-adoption reports came to AAI as per the adoption agreement. According to the adoption agency, everything in the reports seemed normal and Hana had filled out to a healthier 105 pounds. However, in June 2009, the reports suddenly stopped. Although the adoption agreement stated that Carri and Larry would continue to send reports throughout the children's lives, technically they were under no legal obligation to file the reports. The adoption agency had no way of knowing the atrocities that were going on in the Williams household.

Larry and Carri Williams believed in a strict fundamentalist Christian lifestyle. In addition to homeschooling their children, almost all television and Internet access was prohibited. They believed women should never wear pants, only skirts or dresses and never swimsuits, and certainly never vote. The children were rarely seen in a public setting and only socialized with a select few like-minded families. Larry regularly preached to the children in the backyard of their rural five-acre property.

As for disciplining the children, the Williamses adhered to the teachings of a controversial book called *To Train Up A Child* by Michael and Debi Pearl. The book taught that the principles and techniques for training an animal and raising a child were the same. It instructed parents to begin spanking their children within the first few months of birth to "break their will."

In his book, Michael Pearl's argument for beating a child came straight from his interpretation of the Bible. Pearl believed that Proverbs 13:24 justified his beliefs:

> "He that spareth his rod hateth his son."

Pearl said,

> "A child properly and timely spanked is healed in the soul and restored to wholeness of spirit. A child can be turned back from the road to hell through proper spankings."

The book went into great detail of specific implements for parents to use; a wooden spoon, spatula, or the most popular weapon — a short length of small plastic plumbing tubing. This was a particularly well-liked implement because it could be easily curled up and kept available in a parent's pocket at all times. The book also taught parents to withhold food and put children under a cold outdoor garden hose as punishment.

The Pearls' book was extremely popular with fundamentalist Christian homeschoolers and, according to the author, sold almost 700,000 copies in the first seven years of its publication. The Pearls' No Greater Joy ministry generated upwards of $1.7 million tax-free dollars per year.

———

For the next two years, Hana's hopes of the American dream quickly washed away. Life with the Williams family was nothing like the *Little House on the Prairie* life she had envisioned.

Within months after Hana arrived in the United States, she began menstruating. This infuriated Carri, who told members of her knitting group that she had wanted to adopt "a little girl, not a half-grown woman." She complained that Hana was rebellious, telling her knitting friends, "I wouldn't wish her on anyone."

Friends and neighbors of the Williams family had noticed that Hana and Immanuel were often absent from public family outings, holidays, trips to town, or to church. On the rare occasion that they were brought to church with the family, one parishioner that knew sign language often attempted to sign with Immanuel, but Carri and Larry didn't want him communicating with anyone. One of them would quickly whisk the boy away before he had a chance to converse.

Neighbors noticed the seven children would be seen actively playing together at the front of the Williams' home, while Hana and Immanuel would be left standing alone near the driveway staring at their feet.

At home, the discipline was much worse than anyone could have imagined. Hana had Hepatitis B, which again infuriated Carri, who accused her of purposely smearing blood on the bathroom walls. Because of this, Hana was not allowed to use the bathroom in the house. She was only allowed to use a filthy outdoor portable toilet behind the barn that was only serviced twice a year.

The indoor shower was off limits too. Regardless of temperature, Hana's shower was a garden hose propped up with sticks in the front yard. Hana was often forced to use the cold makeshift shower while the other children watched from the windows of the warm house.

When Hana made any sort of complaint about the clothes that Carri had chosen for her to wear, she would lose her right to wear clothes at all, and given only a towel to wear for the day.

Hana had long braided hair that she was proud of. Her hair was the one thing she could take pride in and Carri knew it. The first spring of Hana's new life, she was told to cut the grass in the yard. When she finished, the grass was cut shorter than Carri had wanted it. As punishment, Carri shaved her head. She would later shave her head on two additional occasions.

The daily punishments had begun almost immediately after the children were adopted. Most of the time, Immanuel and Hana had no idea why they were being punished. It could have been for standing in the wrong place or getting an answer wrong on their schoolwork. They were never quite sure.

A few months after arriving in the United States, traumatized by the change of environment and daily punishments, Immanuel began wetting the bed. Carri and Larry were convinced he was doing it on purpose just to anger them. The boy was taken outside and was given a shower with the cold hose, then sent to sleep in the dark shower room.

To add to his trauma, Carri often teased him by running the plastic tubing she called her "switch" up and down his face. On one occasion, Larry hit Immanuel on the top of the head with his fist and caused blood to run down his face. That night, he was made to sleep outside and the other children were told not to sign with him.

The punishments themselves were often straight from the *To Train Up A Child* book and involved beatings with a piece of plastic tubing that Carri kept in her bra. Sometimes it was one of Larry's belts folded in half, or a long, flexible piece of glue stick. Other common forms of punishment that the Williamses adhered to from the book included denying food, denying clothes, forced outdoor sleeping, and cold outdoor showers.

The Williams' biological children were punished, too, but never to the severity of Hana and Immanuel. The adopted children were fed different meals than the biological children. While the other children had sandwiches, Hana and Immanuel would have the same sandwich, but with a glass of water poured over it. Sometimes they would get cold leftovers with unheated frozen vegetables. Almost always, the two children were forced to eat outside while the other children ate inside, regardless of the cold, rain, or snow.

Because of Hana's menstruation, Larry and Carri took the initial steps to change her official age. Carri told her knitting group that if they could get her age bumped up a few years, they could kick her out of the house sooner when she turned eighteen. When another member of the knitting group asked how the girl would survive in the outside world, Carri snipped, "It wouldn't be my problem."

In the three years that Hana lived with the Williamses, she went from sleeping alone in the barn behind the house, to being locked inside a bathroom with no light, to eventually being kept in a four-foot by two-foot closet for up to twenty-four hours at a time. Larry's recorded bible sermons and religious music played outside of the closet the entire time, depriving her of sleep.

———

In the afternoon of Wednesday, May 11, 2011, Carri sent Hana into the backyard as one of her daily punishments. It was a rainy spring day and the temperature was in the mid-forties. When Hana, only wearing shorts and a t-shirt, complained that she was cold, Carri commanded that she do jumping jacks in the yard to stay warm. After a few hours alone outside, the children noticed Hana's lower lip quivering. She seemed unable to control her own movements, had fallen a few times, and eventually had trouble standing up at all.

Carrie went out the back door of the home and grabbed Hana by the arm and led her to the outhouse behind the barn. She continued to fall repeatedly, which infuriated Carri. She believed Hana was only trying to create attention. Unable to get her to stand, Carri left her lying alone in the yard.

Hours later, Hana's clothes were soaked. Carri set dry clothes on the back porch and yelled at her to come back inside the house. When Hana didn't return, Carri called on her two eldest sons. She gave the boys a length of plastic tubing and told them to hit her on her bottom for not following orders. Strangely, as the boys whipped her, she started to remove her own clothing and Carri called the boys back inside. By 5:00 P.M. Hana began throwing herself down on the pavement, gravel driveway, and grass. Her knees and hands began to bloody as Carri watched from inside the warm house. When she couldn't watch anymore, Carri turned away from the window and ignored Hana for the rest of the evening.

Near midnight, the seven biological Williams children giggled as they continued to stare out the window at Hana, who had removed all of her clothing and was still uncontrollably throwing her body around in a fit. She was wallowing in the mud and pounding her own head into the ground. They watched in amusement as Hana was experiencing what's known as "paradoxical undressing." In the final stages of hypothermia, the nerves can become damaged causing irrational behavior. This final stage of hypothermia tricks the mind into thinking it's extremely hot, causing the person to remove their clothes and attempt to burrow themselves into the ground.

When Hana finally stopped moving, one of the daughters called their mother to come check on Hana. She was facedown in the yard with a mouth full of mud. Carri, upset with Hana's nudity, grabbed a bedsheet and wrapped it around Hana. She then instructed her boys to drag her into the house.

First Carri called Larry, who was driving home from work. When she hung up, she finally dialed 911.

> "I think my daughter just killed herself.... She's really rebellious, and she's been outside, refusing to come in. And she's been throwing herself all around. And then she collapsed."

> "Is she breathing?"

> "I don't think so, no."

> "How old is your daughter?"

> "I don't know. We adopted her almost three years ago."

> "You don't know how old she is?"

> "She's somewhere between the ages of fourteen and sixteen. She was throwing herself all over the gravel, the yard, the patio. We went to bring her in. My sons tried to carry her in,

and she took her clothes off. She's very passive-aggressive. I don't know how to describe it."

During the call, Carri sounded more annoyed than saddened or shocked. The 911 operator coached Carri through CPR, but it was no use. Hana was gone. When emergency crews arrived, Hana had a large lump on her forehead and she was covered in blood. Her hips, knees, elbows, and face had fresh red bloody markings from repeated whippings. She also had a stomach infection.

The postmortem examination of Hana's body revealed she was abnormally thin for just thirteen years old. At only five feet tall, she was emaciated and had gone back down to 76 pounds. She was lighter than 97% of girls her age and thinner than she was when she originally came from Ethiopia three years earlier. The official cause of death was hypothermia compounded by malnutrition and gastritis (stomach infection). It was determined that her body had been too thin to retain enough heat on the day she died.

———

When Child Protective Services knocked on the door of the Williams home the following day, Larry refused to let them in. Two weeks after Hana's death, the entire family were interviewed by detectives and Child Protective Services. All the children gave the same story, obviously coached by their parents: Hana was rebellious and "possessed by demons."

When Immanuel was interviewed, he told detectives, "People like Hana got spankings for lying and go into the fires of Hell." When Larry heard Immanuel give that answer, he immediately stopped the interview and took the children home.

Two months had gone by with no charges brought against the Williamses when Child Protective Services received an anonymous tip. Someone claimed that Carri didn't like her adopted children and Immanuel was being treated much like Hana. With that news, CPS worked with detectives and opened a formal investigation. All eight of the Williams children were taken into foster care. During a search of the house, police found a copy of the book *To Train Up a Child*.

Even after months in foster care, Immanuel was afraid of his foster parents and nervously apologized for every little mistake he made, even asking his foster mother why she wasn't beating him. He told his therapists of repeated nightmares and constantly worried that he would be the next to die. Immanuel was diagnosed with post-traumatic stress disorder.

That September, more than four months after Hana's death, Carri and Larry Williams were arrested on charges of homicide by abuse and first-degree manslaughter for the death of Hana, as well as first-degree assault of a child for the abuse of Immanuel.

Carri and Larry each faced a potential life sentence. Both posted bail of $150,000 each, but were given strict orders to not contact each other or any of their children — either directly or through third parties or other means. However, when Larry continued to send highlighted bible verses to the children, the prosecution believed them to be coded messages encouraging them to come to his defense. Larry Williams was arrested again and placed in a state jail where he remained for almost two years awaiting trial.

———

This wasn't the first time that the book by Michael and Debi Pearl, *To Train Up a Child,* had been linked to a child's death. Two other sets of fundamental Christian parents that employed tactics from the book had recently killed their adopted children: Sean Paddock and Lydia Schatz. The three deaths happened in different parts of the United States, but all were adopted, homeschooled, and beaten with a length of 1/4 inch plastic tubing, as recommended by Michael Pearl.

Seven-year-old Lydia Schatz's parents, Kevin and Elizabeth, held her down and beat her for nine hours with a piece of the tubing for pronouncing the word "pulled" incorrectly. Four-year-old Sean Paddock's mother Lynn Paddock smothered him in a blanket wrapped too tightly around him because she wanted to stop him from getting out of bed in the middle of the night. Like Hana, the abuse that eventually killed these children was just the tip of the iceberg.

———

At trial, Carri and Larry turned on each other. The couple sat at opposite tables in the courtroom, rarely looking each other in the eye. Larry testified that the discipline was all at the hands of Carri, while Carri testified that her discipline was at the instruction of her husband. Carri also admitted that she told her children not to talk to detectives about any of the abuse. The children, however, testified that lying was considered one of the most serious offenses in their household.

One of the Williams children, Joshua, confirmed that Hana had not been homeschooled or eaten meals with the other children for at least a year before her death. The child told the court that she would sometimes go two days without anyone speaking to her and none of the biological children liked her, "but it didn't matter because she was always in the closet."

Immanuel testified using sign language with the help of three interpreters. The courtroom was silent as he was asked what he thought happened to Hana. "I don't know" he signed. "She disappeared. I think maybe she's dead." He also testified that he was often beaten with a stick or plastic tubing until blood ran down his face, telling the court, "I would suffer with the pain until it eventually went away."

The biological children admitted that they were coached to tell authorities that Hana slept in the bedroom with them, when in fact she slept in a tiny locked closet. The jury was shown the closet that she slept in and were shown photos of the scars on Hana's body from repeated beatings.

Larry testified that he trusted his wife's discipline choices with the adopted children because she had done such a good job raising the other children. Carri rebutted that her husband was an equal participant in the discipline and even came up with some methods on his own, like hosing off Immanuel and locking him in the shower room after his bedwetting. She also testified that Larry was the one that installed the lock on the closet door.

During the trial, the defense attempted to argue that Hana was actually sixteen-years old rather than thirteen. If she had been sixteen at the time of her death, the homicide-by-abuse charge could not be applied as it only applies to children younger than sixteen.

Since there was no documentation of her birth from Ethiopia that proved her age either way, the trial was post-poned to have Hana's body exhumed for examination. Tests on her teeth and bones, however, were inconclusive and experts couldn't confirm that she was sixteen.

The defense agreed that Larry and Carri may have been bad parents and their choices were bad, but they weren't killers and had no idea that their form of discipline would lead to the child's death.

After seven weeks of testimony, the jury didn't agree with the defense and both Larry and Carri Williams were convicted of first-degree manslaughter and first-degree assault. Carri was also found guilty of homicide by abuse and was sentenced to thirty-seven years in prison. Larry Williams was sentenced to nearly twenty-eight years and given credit for the almost two years he had been in jail awaiting trial.

———

This chapter is a free bonus chapter from True Crime Case Histories: Volume 5

Online Appendix

Visit my website for additional photos and videos pertaining to the cases in this book:

http://TrueCrimeCaseHistories.com/vol4/

More books by Jason Neal

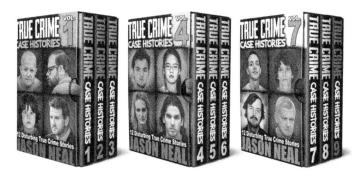

Looking for more?? I am constantly adding new volumes of True Crime Case Histories. The series **can be read in any order**, and all books are available in paperback, hardcover, and audiobook.

Check out the complete series at:

https://amazon.com/author/jason-neal

All Jason Neal books are also available in **AudioBook format at Audible.com.** Enjoy a **Free Audiobook** when you signup for a 30-Day trial using this link:

https://geni.us/AudibleTrueCrime

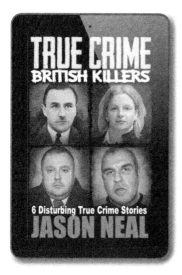

FREE BONUS EBOOK FOR MY READERS

As my way of saying "Thank you" for downloading, I'm giving away a FREE True Crime e-book I think you'll enjoy.

https://TrueCrimeCaseHistories.com

Just visit the link above to let me know where to send your free book!

THANK YOU!

Thank you for reading this Volume of True Crime Case Histories. I truly hope you enjoyed it. If you did, I would be sincerely grateful if you would take a few minutes to write a review for me on Amazon using the link below.

https://geni.us/TrueCrime4

I'd also like to encourage you to sign-up for my email list for updates, discounts and freebies on future books! I promise I'll make it worth your while with future freebies.

http://truecrimecasehistories.com

And please take a moment and follow me on Amazon.

One last thing. As I mentioned previously, many of the stories in this series were suggested to me by readers like you. I like to feature stories that many true crime fans haven't heard of, so if there's a story that you remember from the past that you haven't seen covered by other true crime sources, please send me any details you can remember and I will do my best to research it. Or if you'd like to contact me for any other reason free to email me at:

jasonnealbooks@gmail.com

https://linktr.ee/JasonNeal

Thanks so much,

Jason Neal

ABOUT THE AUTHOR

Jason Neal is a Best-Selling American True Crime Author living in Hawaii with his Turkish-British wife. Jason started his writing career in the late eighties as a music industry publisher and wrote his first true crime collection in 2019.

As a boy growing up in the eighties just south of Seattle, Jason became interested in true crime stories after hearing the news of the Green River Killer so close to his home. Over the subsequent years he would read everything he could get his hands on about true crime and serial killers.

As he approached 50, Jason began to assemble stories of the crimes that have fascinated him most throughout his life. He's especially obsessed by cases solved by sheer luck, amazing police work, and groundbreaking technology like early DNA cases and more recently reverse genealogy.

Printed in Great Britain
by Amazon

39339328R00106